To myself

I thank me for believing in me and this vision.
For investing in myself.
To acknowledging my weaknesses,
but not allowing them to dim my determination.
I thank me for never allowing the negative to deter me to stray from my path.
To my strengths and courage which continue to fuel me.
For never giving up or giving in.
I salute me!

Table of Contents

DEDICATION
ACKNOWLEDGMENTS
PREFACE
CHARLES IS THE NAME, STEPPIN'S THE GAME
LOVE THE ROLL
THERE WAS A TIME
A LOVE, A PASSION TO SKATE
THE OTHER HALF OF ME
HOW IT ALL STARTED FOR ME
MY SKATING JOURNEY
ROLLER SKATING ISN'T A JOB
MEMOIR OF A TREND$ETTA
HOW SKATING SAVED AND IMPACTED MY LIFE
SKATING IS WHO I AM
THE ZEN OF SKATING
THE KING OF SLIDZ
MY SK8 LIFE JOURNEY
THE LIFE OF MSROLLINDIVA
MY SK8 HISTORY
ROLLIN' UNIFIED READY
FOR THE LOVE OF ROLLER SKATING
ROLLO'S STORY
THE UK AND BEYOND
NEW YORK SK8 OF MIND

- [BUTTERFLY SEASON: THE BIRTH OF LADY P](#)
- [THE ROLLER WAVE](#)
- [A SKATING LOVE STORY](#)
- [ROLLER, ROCKER, REVIEW](#)
- [IN MEMORIUM](#)
- [THIS IS MY STORY, MY LOVE STORY A TRIBUTE TO LEZLY ZIERING](#)
- [LIST OF AUTHORS IN CHAPTER ORDER](#)
- [ABOUT THE LEAD AUTHOR](#)

ACKNOWLEDGMENTS

*"When you have a passion for something then you tend not only to be better at it,
but you work harder at it too."*
– Vera Wang

This project was born of love and was divinely guided. It is a masterpiece in the making, a way for us to record our history by relating our very own unaltered stories. This is our voices collectively sharing our passion for this little thing called roller skating. It's, style, class, artistry in motion – a form of expression, an outlet, a friend, it is love, it is life.

A special praise to each person who was courageous and gracious enough to share their story. Also, for being trusting and faithful that I would represent them and the culture with pride and respect, for this I am forever grateful and indebted as I am sure are those who will read this book.

To the tribe of phenomenal skaters, DJ's, skate organizers, videographers, critics, rink owners and all those who make our ride inside and outside the rink enjoyable, know you are all appreciated more than you could ever comprehend. While you may not verbally be graced with our thanks, we understand that your dedication to the skate culture is borne out of love, for the richness received is not that of money but the satisfaction of the smiles on each skater's face as they roll.

I give special praise and acknowledgements to those who visually catalog our artistry - Linwood Neverson of Sk8Kingz Media, Doug Mike of Sk8 Vidzz, Terrance Glover of Triple 7 magazine, Chad Ha of SkateLyfe TV and Tyrone Dennis for your contributions to this project. And to any others who may have contributed and are nameless, I thank you and send prayers and gratitude to all.

For his extensive contributions to the skate community which is unyielding. His unmatched talent and energy, for his insight and love for the preservation of the culture I extend my heartfelt appreciation and gratitude to Ice from Philly, a legend in his own right. Ice you have always been honest, real and humble. I praise you for imparting your knowledge and wisdom about the history of people, the artistry and culture of roller skating, for this I honor you. For believing in my vision from day one and giving your all to help make my vision a reality, I ask blessing be in your favor in this life and in the next. ~ Love and Blessings

To the new, greats and legends in our culture - Jody Allen, Terry Connors, Saladin Suluki, Stormy Scrubb, Denise Wesley, Shedney Matthews, Dr. Pamela Pine, Odis Rowlett, Melvin Bullock, Ash London, Denise Knowles, Sk8Fantacee, Teena Mayes-Moody, Kenneth Purdue, John Perkins, Pete Russell, Lionel Laurent, Angela Parham, Jaye Flynn, Peachie Richardson, Pearl Jewlez Gardner, Shamar Cunningham, Gloria "GloCrazy" Downs, DJ Mook, Patrick of Skate Fever, Kamille Boyd-Gilmore, Nikki Forrester, Rickey Davis, Roger G, Quest Love to Skate, Harry Gaskin, Wykeia Chante, Traci G. Hilton, Ali – El, Paco Holmes, Asha Kirkby, Rick Smith, Alicia Reese, Trish "Jive Biscuit" Cherry, Tony Camacho, Zakee Madyun, Ant Live, Tony Zane, Andrea "MoneyMaker" Ro-Hoodtimes Christopher Banks, DJ Nile, BossLadii FlyyChicc, Tonya Sprott, Tone Rapp Flemmings, Janice Waldner, Naeemah Lamont, Sally-Ann Ball, Van Dex Haynes, Jeron Land, Ronda Ellen Flanzbaum and Christopher White and the list could go on forever.

Forgive me for those not mentioned, charge it to my mind and not my heart, check for your name in Volume III ~ Peace and Blessings.

PREFACE

"Passion is energy. Feel the power that comes from focusing on what excites you."
~ Oprah Winfrey

The Evolution of Skating is a collaboration of tribe members in the skate world. It is a journey of sorts, detailing the introduction, acceptance, growth and mastering of the art and skill. It is the "Evolution" of the skater. You will read the stories of skaters legendary and new, Deejays, Event Coordinators, Videographers, Skate Critics, rink owners - national and international. Each chapter provides a sneak peek inside the life of the individuals and the culture that is revered. It's a sharing of this fun, family friendly, heart pumping, music thumping and sometimes gritty underground but well-known phenomenon that has stood the test of time, roller skating.

A family pastime that has been passed down through the ages, irrespective of race, religion, social or financial status. It's an art that can be enjoyed as a family or alone. It's a stress reliever, fun, exercise, a sport, entertainment and even a life saver to some.

The concept of this book is one of the many loves that had been stagnant in my heart and finally came to fruition with the help of my co-authors. I have provided a platform for each person to tell their journey of what skating has meant to them, with the hopes to inspire, invite, encourage, enlighten and brighten the day of each person who turns the page of this book or listens to their stories via the audio book.

You see this pastime has a long and torrid history that began back in 1735 when the first roller skate was invented by John Joseph Merlin, from Belgium. He debuted his new wheeled shoes in London at a party, but crashed into a mirror, embarrassed but not deterred, he went back to the drawing board.

And in Paris the year 1819, Mr. M. Petitbled, a French inventor patented a three-wheeled inline skate model and in 1863 Mr. James Plimpton designed quad skates according to the National Museum of Roller Skating and this, revolutionized roller skating. Plimpton went on to establish the New York Roller Skating Association and he opened his first skating rink in 1866 at a Rhode Island resort, capitalizing on the social aspect of roller skating, he provided a place for the then young Victorian couples to meet up without being chaperoned, brilliant and wise I'd say.

Roller skating has also been touted as a "valuable form of exercise" by many health officials. It increases the output of muscular energy, stimulating your circulation, while having fun and listing to music. Back in the early days, people would skate to a violin player, flutist, organist and the like. Deejays were not introduced to rinks for quite some time and even then, they started playing tapes from radio players not the traditional Deejays we are accustomed to spinning on turntables in this day and age. The Evolution......

Today this passion for elevating roller skating to heights beyond the norm are being taking on by people in our tribe, members like Reggie Brown, Ice from Philly, Jeri Baskerville and Leo White to name only a few. Leo aka "Quad1" as he is known in the skate world, is on the cusp of designing his very own truck so that skaters who desire to skate on one or two wheels can do so without having to go through the pain staking modifications of the past, ingenious – a beautiful mind. The creation and direction of roller skating has and continues to evolve. It is an ever-changing culture full of history, soul and artistry.

Listen with your heart, engage with you mind, bond with you soul and accept that which is to come, the crafty and inventive.

Peace and Blessing upon you ~ Amirah Palmer

CHARLES IS THE NAME, STEPPIN'S THE GAME

Charles Edwards aka Mr. Charles

Back in the early '70s, I was skating back and forth across the county for quite a while and by doing this I met a few people that I enjoyed skating with, so we decided to form a club (or a crew as the young people call it today). So, we formed this club called the Soul Travelers right here at my house in Burlington, New Jersey.

We always liked to skate with soul, and we loved to travel—so that's where we got the name the Soul Travelers. After some time, the members moved all over the place and were not together as a group anymore, but individually we all still skate. I went to the first eleven skate parties held in Atlanta. The ATL was one of the places that they held a skate party every year, the Sk8-a-Thon and it's still going on today. This will be the twenty-fifth year for the Skat-a-Thon. For the last couple of years, I haven't attended Skat-a-Thon, but a few of the members from different clubs always call me—out of Philadelphia, New York—wherever they are to keep in touch. Skate-a-Thon is a big thing and I think it's even spread to other places, as people began to attend Skate-a-Thon and saw what was going on, we began to see big parties start-up in different regions and states.

Things are pretty good for the skaters; I talk to a lot of them all the time. Well, mostly I've been speaking with Ice from Philly, as he gives you awareness of what's going on with a lot of the people we have known for years.

When I got out of the military, I began to skate all over. I decided, hey, I'm not the only one in love with skating! There's a lot of people out there that don't know much about what skating is all about. I and a few of my friends would get together, do shows at different places around New Jersey. We'd do little skate shows for the schools, churches, or any place to show them there's more to skating than just rolling around and pushing each other down and falling. That was the start of it, and it is still going on—I hope that it never stops. As more people continue learning and follow many of the OG's still skating—the young people will grow and continue the legacy.

There have been so many changes in the skate world since I came along, but as the saying goes, the more things change the more they stay the same. Like a lot like the steps, they do now, we've been doing them for years. I made up skate steps that a lot of people are doing now.

You'll go someplace and see some of the steps going on and some of the people who know me will ask, "Hey, where did this step come from?"

The younger generation doesn't know, but the people who know enlighten them saying, "Hey, that step came from a group in New Jersey, called the Soul Travelers! That's one of their famous steps."

People will take your steps, add a lil' something to it and change the name and say, it's theirs, but as I say there are a million different routines/steps out there and they've been going on a long time. I've skated a lot in California with a close friend of mine named Richard Humphrey and he has tapes of the steps that he developed, even wrote a book about them. He kept the video on everything, he still has a skate club out in California and he's still doing his thing and a lot of his steps are still bouncing around on the internet. At times when we talk, he would say to me that he's gone somewhere and seen people in different places doing some of the same steps that I used to do, that we used to do together. Yes, there are good skaters all over everywhere and I know there are quite a few people who know me because I've skated everywhere—in Chicago, California, Baltimore, Detroit, Atlanta, St. Louis, and all of Ohio.

Starting in late 79-80, our group the Soul Travelers, started traveling to places like New Jersey and Twin City Roller Rink—which was one of the biggest rinks in Jersey. We also went up to New York and became close to those skaters in NY, New Jersey, and Twin Cities. New Jersey had skate parties going on before they started anything on a national scene. We skated for the fun and love of skating. There was comradery, we loved everybody—and enjoyed each other. I feel the skate scene is a lot bigger now. Each time I go to a different city, leave, and come back in about six months—they have formed a skate club there! So now, skaters are pretty much everywhere and I hope skating continues to keep growing.

In the last few years, I haven't been to many skate events because I've had eye surgery, I could see good but my right eye hadn't healed well, but I still talk to my friends and I feel like there may be a shift with the culture. My friends feel like it's a big change, I don't know if the younger people today are as close together as we were. The older groups are still out there and we talk like we have known each other for a million years—like we were more of a close-knit family. The older skaters in our time were much friendlier, but times seem to be changing.

When I was coming up there weren't many skaters that I looked up to here in Jersey. Now, I had friends in Chicago. My aunt lived there, and when I was a kid, I used to see skaters tearing up the floor! Keep in mind, this was a long time ago, we're talking about going back thirty years. They were doing it out there, they did their thing! They had at least six or seven rinks spread out in Chicago. There were lots of skaters out there, and I ended up meeting a lot of people. The windy city's culture was different, and people from different rinks gave entertaining skate parties. In Chicago, Vanessa Poindexter had a newsletter back then and used it to announce up-and-coming skate parties. A few other people I knew in New York, Bill Butler included, was one of the first that had their group organized—and it was a very good group. They used to do shows around New York. This group started going to some of the skate parties or marathons as we called them and people started picking up on his style—the New York freestyle.

So, running into other skaters I met before was really weird! It seemed as if no time went by, as we picked up where we left off at our last meeting, just like it was yesterday. So, whenever I go to San Francisco to talk to Richard Humphrey about his area—it's the same vibe. In Baltimore, I think their whole group split up and currently I don't know anyone. There were big-time people like Big Bob of New York. He was one of the big-time DJs at the time and he was one of the first skate party DJs out in Atlanta with Joi and John at the Skate-a-Thon. We run into these new DJ's and they are really good! Our DJs should be in touch with each other to lean on and keep the skate parties going.

The skate culture now is in somewhat good hands, as there are a lot of great skaters and so many great skate-moves. I have a few pictures from back in the day (the 90s) where they listed some of the moves and things that the people do now—you know—like what they call the slow walk, a different style of slow walking, and all these styles mixed with different kinds of steps have different names across varying states.

Over the years we traveled from state to state and people would see me and say, "Oh no! Here come the Soul Travelers!"

There would be times when we would enter the rink and people would see us, sit down, not skate—and just watch us. Some of my best buddies would say we would skate all around doing all kinds of flips, steps, and moves, and then here you come in the rink and step out in the middle and all the girls would gravitate towards you. They wanted to know what they were doing wrong. Ice from Philly came to the event called Skaters Choice and apologized to me. He said he didn't know the game until he began watching me and understood how I was able to woo the ladies. Ice said he was doing it all wrong. He used to get mad when I would come in the rink and all the ladies would flock to me. Over the years Ice and I became very good friends.

Back in the day, there were no black-owned rinks but we didn't care! Boldly, we went in the white-owned rinks and started doing our moves and all the white people would sit down and watch us. It was similar to *Band Stand*, if you can remember when this came out everyone was watching it, then *Soul Train* came out and took over the viewing audience, that's how it was when we would walk into the white rinks, we just took over and they would fall in place. When we visited different places, we took over because they couldn't do some of the steps we could do—hell sometimes I would just make up new moves when we got on the floor.

I've had a lot of friends, even ladies—come up to me and tell me, "You know, I saw you skating and I wouldn't dare come up to you and ask to skate with you because you were such a good skater."

Some people just develop at a faster pace than others, and I never looked down on people, I always made it a habit that if anyone came to me and asked—I would take the time to show them how to skate. Now, I didn't go around trying to find you! I ain't going to pick out only nice-looking ladies to show how to skate—if you come to me—then I know you really wanna learn how to skate. That's also what started my skating, the ladies. I would come to the rink and see these beautiful ladies. I feel like if you're good at what you do and you're a nice person, naturally the ladies will flock to you. That's natural with me, people see my kindness.

Eric Alston was my big-time buddy back in the day, we won a great big trophy. When I met Eric in New York he was a great skater, flying around the rink, but he never went in the center he didn't do any steps. Eric confessed to me, man the reason I stopped skating was that every time I came to the rink all the ladies would flock to you, all the girls were with you. After that, I started teaching Eric steps. We were together in Ohio and Eric forced me to enter, I didn't want to get in but he talked me into entering the contest and we won first place, I still have the trophy in my garage.

Richard Humphry, my dear friend, has tapes of things we did together. While out skating he would approach a few people in San Francisco and different areas and he asked some of them where did you get that step from and they would tell him some new names and shortly thereafter he told them I know exactly where you got that step from—my friend in New Jersey.

In the 90s, for ten straight years, I went skating at every skate party in every state. I drove my mom's 1995 Cadillac after she passed—she only had 11,000 miles on the car. I put so many miles on it driving across the states. Most people know me by that red Cadillac. The trips were euphoric; imagine a group of five or six close friends traveling across the states, to skate – it was priceless. We even ran into Assistant Mayor Alicia Reese of Ohio, who used to be a skater back then. I picked her up at the airport in New Jersey, we hosted a party where I met her mother and father—a great family! She used to call me every year, she was a grand hostess of many parties, as a matter of fact—oh the memories!

The advice I would impart on the skater today is to visit other rinks in other states. At one time I could almost tell you by watching a skater go around the rink where they were from, the guy or girl would leave the floor and I would say, you are from the East Coast!

Yeah, yeah.
Yeah Freestyle, right, right.
Right, right.
Step out of your comfort zone,
See the skate world!

A fun fact about me that most people don't know is how friendly I am! It is shocking I know—but so many people came to me after they got to know me and say I used to want to come and skate with you but I was scared.

I'm as gentle as they come, but for some reason, you'd never know unless you approach me!

ABOUT THE AUTHOR:

Charles Edwards was Honorably Retired from the U.S. Airforce reaching the rank of Staff Sargent (SSgt). Serving in the fields of Communications and Supply. Charles served two tours in Korea, one in the Philippines and one in Alaska

In his private life as a roller skating phenomenon, he was the winner of multiple awards for stepping. He won singles, doubles and as a group for "Best Steppers" and "Favorite Steppers".

Fun Fact: Charles was a beast on the basketball court and has many awards to prove it.

Facebook: https://www.facebook.com/profile.php?id=100065053062091

QUOTES:
If you try you risk failure, if you don't you ensure it ~Unknown

LOVE THE ROLL

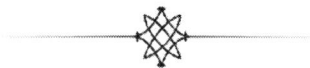

Khannie Butler aka The Scenario

Skating in the streets of Philadelphia since the age of six—I have always loved roller-skating. In 1965, we had the metal skates with the skate key to make physical adjustments to our shoe size and at the time, I was easily a size eight youth. What I loved most at this time was our neighbors were understanding and reveled in our love for street skating.

In those days, I rolled up and down Fletcher Street, 30th Street, and many times throughout the Fairmount Park area in North Philly with my brothers, cousins, and friends from the neighborhood. We had real bonafide connections both family and neighbors. What a joy!

I loved skating during those times because as we rolled through the streets, and in the park, the feeling of life's freedom hit me as the wind blew against my face—skating as fast as I could. This was such a sensation, that not even the sweetest candy could compare to it! Those were the days of just skating without a label or a particular skill, but just being able to roll as fast as you could to keep up with the other fastest skaters. I felt vindicated because I was competitive! At such a young age, I already knew this was going to be my FOREVER CRAFT!

My older cousin, Vanessa Brown, introduced me to the wood floor around 1967. Along with her teenage friends, the eight-year-old version of me would not truly understand that experience until a devastating event happened in my life.

I am the youngest of three children and the only girl. A free-spirit would describe me best as I had an imagination beyond the average eight-year-old because I was going to be the best Director in Hollywood that anyone had ever witnessed. I was going to produce films and make the most beautiful stars shine brightly. That was my dream then. Back then, I was going to produce and make stars like Cicely Tyson, Dianne Carroll, Diana Ross, and so many others stand out in the crowd.

Many of my neighbors enjoyed the fact that I could smile, giggle and spend time alone in the streets close to home—just enjoying life and playing all by myself. There was a lot of freedom in my home because most times, my mother worked two or three jobs at any given time just to ensure that my brothers and I had a roof over our heads and ate three meals a day. The only issue with that was the babysitter was our grandmother who ran a Speakeasy with sordid people filing in and out of her home all hours of the day and night. These were scary times, but my mom had no other option being a single parent.

My grandmother's hustle was a lucrative business and her way of survival, but the wandering eyes of some of her customers made the environment unsafe for a sprightly nine-year-old.

July 1968 was the turning point of my life.

Having returned from swimming at the 30th and Ridge Avenue Street Pool in Philadelphia with my brothers and cousins—I had to run to the bathroom! The restroom door was partially opened (nothing unusual in this house), as I was relieving myself, one of my grandmother's customers entered the bathroom. My swimsuit was around my ankles, I tried to pull the suit back up when he entered, but I didn't move fast enough. This man pounced on me and tried pinning me down without warning, we struggled and somehow fell in the bathtub. This devilish, bastard quickened his attack — he was all over me. His heavy breathing was like an oppressive humidity-filled day swallowing me up, as he tried to rape me. I fought with all my might, but at least two inches of his penis penetrated me before I fought him off enough to get away.

Running to the 3rd floor of my grandmother's home where my aunt Janet lived—**I screamed, "Aunt Janet help me! That man tried to, he tried to, he tried to..."**

I didn't even know what happened. But, after I described to my aunt what happened, she immediately knew the man raped me.

My dad and many others looked for the worthless degenerate—but to no avail. However, the police caught up to him, because he had a warrant from North Carolina for raping two sisters.

There was a trial and this dirty bastard received sentencing of only seven years in jail. However, the long-lasting effect that it left on my life was devastating. What was most distressing about that event was the freaking defense attorney practically blamed ME for seducing my rapist! I'm nine, what the hell do I know about seducing anybody? Sexualizing black girls at an early age was clearly this lawyer's dodge—and is a racist and sexist part of society that is still with us today.

After years of being a rebellion and a runaway. Yes, I was spiraling out of control and the only salvation was to return to the skating rink at the age of fourteen around 1973. Riding a bus, subway, and trolley to Elmwood skating rink on Tuesday nights from 8 –11 PM. in the Southwest section of Philly where black folks were not welcome. The bus, subway, and trolley rides to that rink were scary—but I persevered to do what I loved! Saturday nights from 7 PM–10 PM at Carman Gardens Roller Skating Rink in the Germantown section of Philly was the place to be with all the, in my head, stars of Roller Skating would venture. This was my only salvation to peace.

I realized when traveling to Elmwood, the white folks hated us! But skating was my passion and I did not give a damn what I had to do to roll. I had to forget about the hate they had for us and stay focused on my goal, which was skating. Skating, skating, skating—that is all I ever wanted in life back then! It was better than the sun!

On a Tuesday night in 1975, some skaters and I were on the Number 36 trolley on our way home from skating (Elmwood Roller Skating Rink). While the trolley sat at a red light, several white men approached and began throwing bottles and sticks at our trolley. Jesus that was a scary experience! I remember this skater, I think his name was Gary, he pushed all the women (black women and skaters) to the back of the trolley, pulled out a gun, and told those white men to BACK THE HELL OFF!!! They did and he became my hero! Nothing could stop me from my love for the ROLL! I was back on that trolley the next week.

Of course, there continued to be a series of encounters with these hateful white men until one Tuesday night I was having a conversation with a few female skaters who lived just across the bridge to the left of Elmwood and alerted me of another route to take to the rink which included a predominately black neighborhood. What? This revelation changed my life. I was taking the wrong trolley to the rink. Now the year is 1976, I am happily taking Trolley Number 11 to skate, and all was well. No more incidents with the mean-spirited whites.

In the initial days of attending skate sessions at Carman Garden Rolling Skating Rink, I would just sit in the corner and watch whomever I considered the 'greatest skaters alive.' One of them was my sister-in-law, Crystal Green Moore. A phenomenal skater and she won a few trophies for being one of the best to do her thing. She was smooth as ice. Someone really should have recorded her moves on video! Her stride compares to no other. God as my witness, that woman could roll! Although she hung up her skates many years ago, she still cheers me on from the sidelines.

My now sister-in-law was my best friend.

Funny story: She and I would skate all over the city attending too many events to name, but the main reason we bonded was our love for the roll. We skated every night except Mondays. Hmmm, thinking back, Monday night Gospel sometimes was on our agenda.

One night, I was at my eldest brother's house begging for money to skate, nothing unusual since I was nineteen years old and didn't have a care about the value of a dollar when I heard some giggling and low-sounding talk coming from my brother's bedroom. I opened the door and discovered my best friend, Crystal, making out with him! What a shocker. They are a couple and I didn't even know. I think I was more disappointed in the secrecy as opposed to them being a couple. Uggh! Ok, I'm over it. I just needed the $4.00 to get in the rink and buy a burger and an orange soda at the McDonald's down the street after skating. I'll deal with Crystal later.

Even with the discovery of the relationship between Crystal and my brother, we remained skate partners and best friends. We did some crazy dips on slow skate that had folks talking for years. Young skaters incorporated that style into their rotation today. I bet they don't even know who some of the contributors of that move are—but I can say Crystal and I mastered it! There is no doubt it will be forever embedded in my memory bank.

Crystal's MS (multiple-sclerosis) put her out to skate pasture, but she rose from those ashes to become one of the most creative, strongest, and God-fearing women I know. I love her so much!

While I experienced many failed relationships, including marriage, I held on to what made me the happiest, ROLLER SKATING.

In 1976, as I began building my love for the roll, I eventually came out of the corner at Carman's and hit the floor like this craft was made especially for me! I enjoyed fast backwards. I still get a kick out of people staring at me in awe because it appeared that I came from nowhere exhibiting a particular skill when unbeknownst to them, I was also skating on Saturday and Sunday afternoons perfecting slow and fast backwards skate. I made many friends quickly and was immediately invited into the circle that my now sister-in-law was a member. Yes, my sister-in-law was first, my best friend! We formed a friendship a couple of years before she met my brother. It is funny; I did not even know they were a couple until they were in love. Ok, so they married on November 7th, 1981.

Throughout the years of skating up and down the 95 corridors from Elsmere in Delaware, Franklinville in New Jersey, Wheel-A-While in Maryland, and of course all the rinks visited in Philly where I grew up, I met so many amazing skaters along the way.

It wasn't until the year 1991 when I moved to the DMV (DC, MD and VA), many skaters began to know my name. I didn't even know it. Skaters were calling me one of the fastest female skaters to hit the floor. WOW!

I was in and out of a couple of clubs, including Rollers Unlimited. That organization changed my perspective of how I viewed friendships. We were and still are a true family. We looked out for one another on and off the skate floor. We are family. Marriages, children, education, job accomplishments, military commitment, deaths and so much more. We hold each other up for love.

In 1998, Trilogy was born. This was a party developed to keep the immediate tri-States skaters connected. DC, MD, VA, PA, DE, NJ and NY.

In early 1999, the name Trilogy would retire to a place of honor—and the birth of a new name came forth—THE SCENARIO!

Scenario was making its own name brand standout as I continued to find myself. In Missouri around 2001 where Marilyn Moore, my daughter, and partner in crime, and I connected with another sisterhood that included Patrice Koonce and her club (KCMO Roll Patrol). In the short time that I lived in Missouri (six months), they embraced Marilyn and me like family. Always looking out for us. True story; one Thursday night while skating at their regular session, I lost the key to my locker but didn't realize it until the end of the night. I went to what I thought was the locker and it was open revealing an empty space. I immediately went to Patrice because my shoes, coat, and purse were missing.

This woman took out a gun and said, "NO ONE IS LEAVING UNTIL MY SISTER'S BELONGINGS HAVE BEEN FOUND!"

The rink was under her command until one of the rink guards discovered a key laying on the floor that fit the locker my belongings were in (oops, I must have dropped it during the session). Ok, so no one died or got arrested. Another skate family for life!

Back to The Scenario. It would become a household name that attracted skaters from all over the country and abroad.

My daughter, Marilyn, and I forged an unbreakable partnership in 2004 that took this party to another height, and what a blessing!

As my daughter and I embarked on many skating events, including, Rolling in the Carolinas, Alabama, Chicago (Sherrie Hayes and D-Breez), JiveBiscuit in Atlanta, Tugger Productions in New Jersey, New York Experience, Synergy on the Beach in Virginia and so many more, we welcomed many new skate relationships and engaged in conversations with skaters who shared our same passion for the love of the roll. It was invigorating!

I praise God all the time for keeping me focused and in love with the reason I was able to forgive the man who raped me, but able to rejoice in knowing, IT WAS NOT MY FAULT!

Skating has brought me to many heights of love, enjoyment, devastation, excitement, sisterhood, and happiness.

From 1998 – 2018, for the Scenario, it has been a pleasure to see the faces of skaters entering the buildings where we hosted an event that brought skaters from all over the world to enjoy, engage and appreciate the craft that we all share.

As I turn the corner of my new life, (oh, that!)—figuring that out now is a challenge—as skating is fading quickly into the sunset for me. I hope to revitalize skating again because it has ALWAYS been the center of my life!

I love some of our new skaters, but the only advice I want to offer to them is, stay true to the craft, don't fight over who is the best, and keep rolling! If you battle, keep it FUN! We are all unique and contribute many variations to this sport.

I can remember that loud, annoying clock ticking away on the nights that I couldn't skate for many reasons. Whether the car broke down, I couldn't get a ride, the flu, my mommy wasn't a team player and so many more impeding stories. Memorizing the schedule, damn it's 'ladies only,' ooooh, 'it's couples only,' Oh My God, 'trios,' I love trios! Thinking to myself, I'm not there, they couldn't be having that much fun without me! Thank God there were no social media back in the '70s because I would have needed therapy for all the great times I was missing. That fuzzy feeling that bubbles up inside you when you can't go skating is devastating and that's the reason why we need to keep this craft/hobby going to infinity and beyond!

My story is my truth and if there is anyone out there who needs to share privately, I am here for you.

In closing, if you love roller skating, smile, embrace it, enjoy, teach, mentor, and keep the circle going!

Peace and Blessings!
Khannie 'The Scenario' Butler

ABOUT THE AUTHOR:

Khannie Butler is and Administrative Assistant and Financial Coordinator for a high school in Newark, DE for the last 16 years. She is an influencer with at-risk-students and empowers them to think about their challenges.

She is the founder of the Scenario skate party which ran for 20 years, hosted by Silver and Gold Unlimited.

Ms. Butler's goal is to retire in the next 3 years. She constantly aspires to be better in spirit, health and financially.

She is currently working on her autobiography and hopes to complete it by August 2021. Khannie is the mother of an educated daughter who served in the US Airforce for 10 years. She also encourages and teaches young skaters throughout the US and serves as a mentor to many.

A fun fact about Khannie is that she loves dipping pretzels in orange soda!!

Facebook: https://www.facebook.com/KhannieSGU

QUOTE:

"When they go low, we go high." ~Michelle Obama

THERE WAS A TIME

Lisa Campolo Goodheart

Four decades ago, I belonged to the Philadelphia roller-skating community. Might seem like I was an odd and unlikely member of that community. You're wrong to mistake me for an outsider or a tourist. Taught and mentored by the best? Yes, I was!

Growing up in a suburb of Philadelphia, I was not involved with skate culture. My childhood hobby was riding horses and competing in horse shows. Then I went to college in Massachusetts and returned to Philly for law school in the mid-1980s. At that time, my name was Lisa Campolo, taking jazz dance classes for exercise and fun. Roller-skating had yet to come into my life.

My introduction to roller-skating came through Center City Dance Studio. A skater with a popular jazz dance company there invited me to check out the street skaters. They gathered at Penn's Landing on Sundays to practice routines to music in front of a crowd. Amazed by what I saw, I wanted to do it myself! So, I gave it a try.

After borrowing some skates, I started practicing in a local park. Following my law school classes, I learned to stay on my feet and start and stop. Then skate forward and backward, to do crossovers and simple spins. Since I always loved dancing, I was able to pick up the moves pretty fast. I became a Sunday regular at Penn's Landing, and I started doing local dance-skate shows with a group that met there.

That's where I met Clyde 'Ice' McCoy, from Philly. His personality, sense of humor, and entertaining style on wheels made me want to watch and learn from him. There was an open spirit to the Philadelphia skate culture that Ice introduced me to in the mid-80s. Along with a kind of wit and energy that I loved! Ice was a great teacher, and we became skating partners and friends for life. We did a skating routine that he put together. Some of the moves are choreographed and some of it free styled and improvised if needed. We had a vocabulary of moves, so Ice could call out the steps and make up the dance as we went along. Depending on what was happening with the music and whatever struck his mood. We did a little bit of stepping, some Lindy, hustle, cha-cha, and tap. A few spins and splits, always with a lot of handclaps. The music was always super-funky. Ice took me under his wing and taught me a lot, especially about showmanship and playing to the crowd.

We started performing as a roller-skating duo in 1986 under the name 'High Energy.' We did the Africamericas Festival Talent Show at the Uptown Theater on Broad Street. After that, we started getting some attention from the local media. The Philadelphia Daily News ran a feature article about us. A local TV station did an evening news feature. Another TV station did a segment on our skating partnership for an entertainment program. We received a citation from the Philadelphia Cultural Council. It was for our contribution to the arts in the city. I remember the two of us doing a little skate demo at the Mayor's press conference. We tried our best to roll on the plush wall-to-wall carpet in the press room at City Hall.

The press attention was about how an odd and unlikely pair we were. As one story put it, "He grew up in the rowhouse ravines of South Philadelphia; she in a rambling Philadelphia suburb cradled by lush lawns and shade trees. He's black. She's white. Together, their differences blur into a whirl of roller-skating mastery, show biz sparkle, and style."

Yeah, yeah, yeah. As far as it concerned us, we were two friends who loved to skate together and have a good time. We didn't let anything – including our obvious differences – get in the way of that.

The media attention that we attracted led to a lot of performing opportunities for Ice and me. We soon expanded our act to include other skaters. Including the founding members of an inactive skate group from North Philly known as the Wizards on Wheels. We all met to skate at JFK Plaza, by the LOVE statue near City Hall. With Ice leading the group, we started learning routines and doing shows like the Wizards on Wheels. At that point, the Wizards consisted of six guys – Ice, Shorty, Anson, Tex, Fudd, and BayBoy – and me.

Performances by the Wizards on Wheels featured rhythmic freestyle solos and duos. We each took turns doing our best bits and tricks out front at center stage. While the others egged us on and marked the rhythm with some simple steps in the backline. This came after our choreographed routines. We performed in unison to open our shows. Some of the guys were break-dancers and poppers, and others were incredible spinners. Then there were the ones that did amazing tricks, and some were stuntmen and daredevils on wheels. I threw in some dance steps, including my renditions of the wop and the cabbage patch, and did my best to keep up.

Ice would have me do a double-handed Lindy slide through his legs. Then come back up, turn around and go down into a split. At which point he would skate over me, stop, come back, and pull me up to a standing position again. Sometimes he would get down on one knee so I could fling a leg across his shoulders. Then he would stand up and spin us both around. With me sitting up top and both of our arms stretched out in parallel lines for balance. He always stopped with ease and set me down in safety and with no trouble, which – believe me – I appreciated! I never developed the skate chops that some of the guys had. Yet the little girls, who showed up at our events, were always very encouraging. That made it fun for me to be part of the show!

When we started together, our outfits were custom-tailored red and navy track pants. Worn along with t-shirts that featured our cartoon images and our names. The letter airbrushed in blue and red graffiti-style. We are thankful to Dave Sims of Creative Visions on Germantown Avenue. Later, we all had personalized blue and gold tracksuits that said 'Wizards on Wheels.' We wore our roller skates unlaced and open, with the tongues hanging out. It was a miracle they stayed on our feet that way.

For me, music was always the thing. This was back before music streaming and even before the invention of CDs. So, finding the funkiest music that fit what we did require some knowledge and research. Homemade mix-tapes played on a rectangular boom box. It was the size of a suitcase is generally what we do. Always looking for something new. Sometimes there would be a DJ at our performances. For parades, the guys would sometimes hook the boombox up to a giant speaker covered with shag carpet. Often powered by a car battery and mounted on wheels. Though it wasn't pretty, it did the trick. It moved along with us, and it never ran out of juice. We skated to Public Enemy, Spoonie Gee, Davy D, KRS-One, D. Nice, and EPMD. The best rolling was always to the rappers of the day, James Brown, Prince, and Michael Jackson. Then whatever else Ice could find that would make us want to move. *Let's Dance to the Drummer's Beat* still sticks in my head as one of our go-to favorite songs. I don't have a cassette tape player anymore. I have

Ice's Easter Def-Rap-Club-House-Mix archived with other irreplaceable time capsules.

We liked to skate at different rinks. Together we have gone to Pennsylvania, New Jersey, Delaware, and Maryland. I remember going to the Elmwood Roller Skating Rink in Southwest Philly. The rink in Bergenfield, by the Teaneck exit off the Jersey Turnpike, in particular, I enjoyed. Even if we weren't performing, we would skate until exhaustion and soaked with sweat. I love to see rink skaters hugging the wall, going fast backward, and moving in tight, close trains. I also love to see the skaters in the middle of a rink, slow-walking in groups or watching each other do their tricks. I watch that stuff on YouTube now – thanks to all the people who follow and film the skaters and post those videos.

The Wizards on Wheels performed at festivals and parades. Also at promotion events, talent showcases, skate parties, and nightclubs. During my time with the group, we had a lot of performances all over the Philadelphia area. At one point, we even did a film commercial for Myers' Rum. Our popularity grew after two different radio stations sponsored us. At the same event but two separate performances. Recently, I found an old calendar and saw that we performed several times a month for a while. At that time, I was working very hard and putting in long days. As a young lawyer making her way in the litigation department of a big law firm. Ice was working nights in a university hospital. The rest of the guys were doing various other things. Looking back, I'm not sure how we managed to coordinate the logistics of everything. Especially with the practices and the traveling around. We wanted to do it bad enough, so we made it work.

A few of the shows I did with the Wizards on Wheels stand out in my memory. One was the City of Philadelphia's Unity Day celebration. Located on the Benjamin Franklin Parkway in the summer of 1987. We started that morning with a warm-up practice at JFK Plaza. Then we skated down towards the Art Museum. It was a beautiful August day and the crowds were huge and very supportive. We did four shows for WDAS-FM radio on the Parkway that day, and we had a ball. A television crew from WPVI-TV followed us around all day. Several other TV channels filmed us, too. It still makes me smile to watch that old video footage.

Another show I remember well was a showcase. It was at the studio of a Philadelphia talent agency. It felt like a great show that night. Everybody was very pumped up and the pace was very fast. There was also a lot of yelling and cheering. We couldn't all fit in the small performing area. So, we worked in a very tight formation, a front line and a backline that kept switching places. We had a new routine choreographed to Michael Jackson's *I'm Bad*. Then segued into *Drummer's Beat* for the solos. Ice had to keep ad-libbing and calling out extra bridge steps to fill some spaces in the music. Which made our big group moves would hit at the right points in the song. Everyone seemed calm, happy, and having fun. We ended our last move right where it needed to be, on the very last beat of the song. It seemed as if the whole thing was on purpose. It felt like magic!

An indelible memory I have of us was winding up with Ice and a skater named Greg at a Center City diner. It was after dancing on skates at the old Second Story nightclub, at 12th and Walnut Streets. Well into the wee hours of the morning following a Halloween Saturday night. The place was super crowded with all these clubbers in Halloween costumes. The atmosphere was brightly lit and loud, with a lot of buzz and energy.

Ice asked this guy at the counter, wearing a dapper double-breasted blue suit, "Say, man, what is your costume supposed to be?"

He said, "I am dressed up as Billy Dee Williams."

He then complained loudly and became bitter. At the same length that he had the Jheri curl, he had the suit, and he had the Colt-45 malt liquor (which "works every time!" according to the TV ad with Billy Dee that was popular at the time), but the get-up wasn't working for him. (You'll have to ask Ice for the rest of the story, but it had us laughing until our sides hurt.)

I had to leave the Wizards on Wheels when I left Philadelphia and moved to Boston in the spring of 1988. At our last show together, the guys surprised me with a going-away gift – a gigantic skate trophy that I ended up carrying on the plane to Boston with me because it was too enormous to fit in my luggage. I had to laugh when I heard that some of them had successfully broken into the trophy store to pick it up, even though it had already gotten paid for because the store closed by the time they got there on the evening of the show.

After I left, the Wizards went on to do many amazing things and accomplished much more on wheels, over the years. I may have been the first woman in the group, but I wasn't the last. I heard a lot of great things about the incredible Linda Corley, who joined the Wizards on Wheels sometime after my departure. She skated with the group for more than a decade. Meanwhile, I found a great new dance community when I moved to

Boston, but I never found a skate scene that was anything like what I had known and loved in Philadelphia.

It was a long time ago and it only lasted for a short time for me, but being a member of the Wizards on Wheels turns out to have been one of the great adventures of my life. I skate pretty rarely now, and I have to take more care when I do, to avoid breaking any (more) of my brittle old-lady bones. Even so, every once in a while, I am inspired to prove to myself – or show my kids – that I can still pull off a few of the old steps. I can't explain the kind of lightness, energy, and joy that comes from dancing on eight polyurethane wheels to a song with a funky beat, when the bass is thumping —and you know all the words! All the while you're laughing and moving in sync with a group of friendly people, just enjoying your day in the sun.

Thanks for everything, Ice.

ABOUT THE AUTHOR:
Lisa Campolo Goodheart entered the skating world when she was a law student in Philadelphia. She got introduced to skating through Center City Jazz Dance Studio in the mid-1980s. The studio was a hangout for a well-known skate-performer. Once Goodheart got a pair of roller skates, she learned some steps, tackled floor work, and became a skater. Lisa became a close friend and skate partner of Clyde 'Ice' McCoy from Philly. She skated with him and Philadelphia's Wizards on Wheels until she moved to Boston in 1988. Goodheart currently is a senior partner in the Boston law firm of Sugarman, Rogers, Barshak & Cohen, P.C. She handles environmental and land use cases. She's married to her great husband for over twenty-six years and is most proud of their two adult daughters, who are theater artists.

lisagood@comcast.net
Twitter - @LisaGoodheart

A LOVE, A PASSION TO SKATE

Jeffrey Hart

My love for skating started at an early age thanks to the man who became my step-father. My passion to skate in the Roller Derby came from my brother who is six years my elder. My soon to become step-father would take us skating every Tuesday night as he courted my Mom. Every Tuesday evening, he would show up at our home to take us to the Elmwood Skating Rink in Southwest Philadelphia for Family Night skating. Mr. Al, as we called him before their marriage, had skating skills and my Mom could skate well enough to get around especially as he held her in his arms. My brother was a natural at most sports activities and was able to skate with speed. I on the other hand had to learn at age four.

Each week I was getting a little better and can remember the first Tuesday night I didn't fall all night and I told everyone whom I knew. Two years after the Family Night skating started my Mom married Mr. Al and the Tuesday night outings stopped because of his work schedule. Now, my brother and I began going to Elmwood every Saturday afternoon as more and more African Americans began coming to the predominantly white attended skating rink. Every Saturday roller skating, and every Sunday ice skating after Church Sunday School. Skating was turning into my life; however, street skates did not appeal to me, as I only skated on them for a short while. I needed to skate on a roller-skating smooth floor inside rather than outside on the rough street. By going to the skating rink weekly my brother had mastered skating backward, doing dance moves to the music, and going fast while I was struggling not to fall going forward. But, my absolute love to skate made me never give up. and I was able to skate.

Two years later my brother went to Virginia for the summer and I, along with neighbor friends, continued the Saturday afternoon skating adventure. When my brother returned, he schooled me on a new sport he had seen on television and informed me that he and I were going to join this sport related to skating. He showed me Roller Derby and a passion to become a professional Roller Derby Skater began. From that moment on everything was I am going to become a Skater in Roller Derby. Two years after my career choice we moved to a home from an apartment and the basement became my roller rink. There was a semi-smooth cement floor that I could skate on like a roller rink and practice Roller Derby. My new neighborhood friends knew me from school and already had heard I was the 'Roller Derby Kid' a name given to me because of my constant talk about becoming a skater. Along with my story of becoming a skater came my slogan, I've got things to do and places to go to become a Roller Derby Skater. I grew up watching Roller Derby which featured competitions of the San Francisco Bay Area Bombers and all talk about becoming a skater meant going to San Francisco. By this time, I was obsessed with skating and joining the Roller Derby and declared to everyone that I was going to be a professional skater. My dearest and closest aunt heard me talking about joining the Roller Derby so much—that she began purchasing me a pair of skates every Christmas until I finally began skating professionally.

My love to skate had turned into a passion that became an obsession. When I walked, I acted as if I was skating, running up the stairs at school or wherever I would run doing the five-five strive learned from watching Roller Derby. Derby skated on a forty-five-degree angled banked track and the way to skate the track was by doing the five-five stride. I learned the five-five stride at the roller and ice rinks, skating in the basement, running up winding stairs, and, skating outside with my boot skates; not street skates. Skating and Roller Derby were all I seemed to live for daily. By this time after four years of wanting to become a professional skater watching Roller Derby, I came across another banked track skating sport called Roller Games. Roller Games didn't excite me as much as Roller Derby, folks were skating men against men and women against women, but the game seemed different to me. Derby and Games were contact sports that were different than going to the roller rink. Friends in the neighborhood and at school started skating and going to the roller rink with me. Of course, I wanted to play Roller Derby while many of them were on skates for the first time and struggled to just stand up, but we had started a regular fun outing and it was roller skating. Roller Skating was all I wanted to do whenever possible.

Watching Roller Derby was as regular as watching a weekly soap opera for me. Now, there was Roller Derby and Roller Games to watch where both league's featured teams located on the West Coast, Derby had the San Francisco Bay Area Bombers, and Los Angeles had the Thunderbirds meaning I still needed to get to the other side of the country if I wanted to become a professional skater. My older brother pointed out to me that both teams only had one African American male and female skater on the good guys and gals' team. I had become a fan of the only Black guy on the Bombers Dewitt Quarles along with the other featured stars Tony Roman, Charlie O'Connell, Dave Battersby, Joan Weston, Carol Meyers, and watched the only Black female on the team, the rookie Dorothy Lee. On the T-Birds, there were only one Black male and female just like Derby "Little" Richard Brown and Ruberta Mitchell.

I can remember the excitement I had when I saw the first Black coach in Derby on television George Copeland skating hard against the Coach of the Bay Bombers Charlie O'Connell, then, I can remember the sheer joy of seeing the first Black female captain, Darlene Anderson, skating against Joan Weston. It seemed every team had at least one African American female and male on their teams. I wondered if I had a chance as a Black guy but never gave up wanting to skate. Roller Games showed me the second Black coach I saw, John Hall and he had the same African American female on his team I saw in a Derby game, Darlene Anderson. They were together on the same team with other Black skaters. I was happy to see the other skaters of color and my brother pointed out to me that the African American leadership was on the team with other Blacks called the Devils. It was a blow to me mentally, but still, I was going to skate professionally and make my way to the west coast to achieve my passion to skate.

Still, with my commitment to skate, I continued to go to roller rinks and watch Roller Banked Track Competition. When Roller Derby came to the Philadelphia area my step-dad took my brother and me to the game in Camden, NJ 1963, and again the next year when they came to the Philadelphia Civic Center. I can remember the day a neighbor informed me that Philadelphia was getting a Roller Games team. As I was not especially a fan of Roller Games I did not keep up with their televised games. What all my skating daily to get to the west coast, now it was coming to Philly. Along with friends I went to the first game that featured Buddy Atkinson, Jr., Judy Arnold, 'Dynamite' Mike Gammon, Judi McGuier, and 'Little' Richard Brown on the Eastern/Philadelphia Warriors skating against Jim 'The King' Trotter: Black coach, Shirley Hardman; Women's Captain of the Texas Outlaws. Professional roller Banked Track Roller Skating coming to Philadelphia; it was great.

Seeing the games in Philadelphia only made my passion grow stronger, now, I would not need to travel to the west coast and a soon as I became sixteen, the starting age to attend training school I would start training to make my childhood dream come true it was now the Fall of 1967 and I was still skating as much as possible feeling the passion to become a professional skater. I went to as many games as possible (weekly), continued to skate everywhere I could rinks, my basement, and, in the street with boot skates.

My love for skating and becoming a professional skater was drawing nearer and in closer reach rather than across the country on the west coast. I knew I had to keep good grades in school to go to the games and to the roller rinks, therefore, I did my best to stay above a 'C' average. I needed to maintain my grades, do my house chores and I would be able to go to banked track skate training.

On my sixteenth birthday, I went to my Mom and Step-Dad to ask them to sign the papers for the Roller Games training. I had followed the instruction given on television about getting the documents to attend training and all I needed was for my parents to sign. With some reluctances they signed and now I would not just be at roller rinks skating I was going to training to fulfill my childhood dream. I started training on October 30, 1970, at the Philadelphia Arena. I can see myself today, getting on the track back then I remember the exact spot on the track I approached ready to do the five-five endeavor I had watched and mastered walking upstairs and skating on flat tracks. Complete joy was all over me as I started skating on the bank track for the first time. what a difference from the flat floors of the roller rinks, now, I was leaning to the side and skating with the same motion going around a Roller Derby track using the five-five stride. After seven months of training moving from the beginner's class to the A-class within two months, I was on my way to the junior league for three months before skating my first professional game on October 31, 1972. My first game was with the Texas Outlaws in Baltimore, MD at the Baltimore Civic Center.

Was I dreaming? Skating on the banked track in front of a crowd with a Texas Outlaws uniform on skating with others I had trained with and some of the biggest stars in the league. GM/Coach Lester Quarles and several others I had watched since I was a youngster, I was now on the track skating with and against. Jim 'The King' Trotter, 'Little; Richard Brown, Otis Williams, Vinnie Gandolfo, etc. Buddy Atkinson became the top selection to skate, taking the infield for the Warriors. I was one proud brother at seventeen and still attending West Philadelphia High School in my senior year. The second game I skated was at the Philadelphia Arena home of the Warriors and where everyone I knew from training school would see and judge me. In the second game, I suffered an injury—receiving three stitches over my left eye when Vinnie Gandolfo did a nutcracker on me and the edge of the helmet sliced me over the eye.

From the track, I and Patti Caven, who was also stricken by injury in the women's field earlier, were on our way to Presbyterian Hospital. The next night I skated the last game of the Texas series, then, went back to the junior league. The second week back in the junior league we were skating at the Philadelphia Spectrum and they announced that two skaters one from the female and one male skater would undergo selection to skate on the Philadelphia Warriors. That night I became the top scorer for my team and subsequently made the Philadelphia Warriors. I skated on the Philadelphia Warriors from that November until June when I elected to go to Hawaii to be on the Hawaiian Warriors. What a whirlwind week I graduated from High School, received the 1971-72 East Coast Rookie of the Year Award, and had the privilege of going to Hawaii for skating.

From that moment on I was skating everywhere and enjoying traveling, meeting other skaters, meeting fans of the game, and growing up living on the road. From Hawaii I came back to Philly for a week and was on my way to Puerto Rico for three weeks, then, to Canada from the east to the west for a month, then, to Cleveland to skate on the home town Bucks, then, to Baltimore to rejoin the Texas Outlaws with Lester Quarles, Larry Lewis, and Ken Adame. I skated with Texas for that series before I was given the news of staying in town to join the Detroit Devils for the next two weeks before we went on our Christmas break. While on break. another notification came down that I was starting the next year on the NY Bombers with Larry Lewis as a coach. Lewis was one of the very best and I had skated with him before as the leader of Texas.

Skating my love and passion in life was actually happening and I was living my childhood dream. I skated the 1973 season with the NY Bombers going to Hawaii, Puerto Rico, and all parts of Canada again and traveling to Japan. Skating took me across the sea and throughout America. My passion was paying off more than I had imagined. I was able to do various skating tricks and bring out many talents on my skates. I learned how to skate with the differences of the skate axle for a banked track skater which is so very different from a flat track skater or dance skater.

I would imagine that a dance skater and bank track skater may adjust their axels in the same fashion making unusual moves in certain skating situations.

I have given a short description of my Love and Passion for skating which occurred at a very young age, me. I was blessed to have the opportunity to become a part of an entertaining sport that showcased skating.

Soon I will be writing a book and in the next installment of my complete story of skating in the Roller Derby/Games going on the road, the actual inside story of the game itself, the history, and the crazy travel moments and hotel stay. Hopefully, this short piece will inspire anyone who may want to skate in any genre of skating they wish speed skating, bank track skating, agility skatin or dance skating.

ABOUT THE AUTHOR:
 Jeffrey Hart is from Philadelphia and has been an avid roller skater since the age of 4 years. His childhood dream to be in the roller derby came to fruition when his parents allowed him to enter Derby training at the age of 16. Jeffrey entered the Derby life and was a part of many teams such as the Texas Outlaws, the Detroit Devils and the NY Bombers. His passion of being a derby skater took him all the United States and internationally fulfilling many of his childhood dreams.
 Jeffrey Hart will soon write an autobiography detailing his Roller Derby Years.

Facebook: https://www.facebook.com/jkhart1021

QUOTE:
You can't fake passion.

THE OTHER HALF OF ME

Israel Jacob Strong aka IsTheWiz

Skating started when I received my first set of skates. My godmother gifted them to me and I will be forever grateful. I received a set of plastic skates made for toddlers when I was two. Although I may have inherited skating from my mother, as she had a deep love for the craft—there was something more to my skating. Growing up, I only had my father and Godmother in my life. My mother was a drug addict and wasn't around much to raise me. This plays a large part in the problems I have today. Currently, I suffer from a major depressive disorder. It's a difficult time dealing with the day-to-day due to unresolved childhood trauma. In many ways skating saved my life. I still got into a bit of trouble but was spared by the grace of God. My troubles didn't lead me to face any legal charges. One thing I do know is if I didn't have skating in my life things would've been much worse.

My godmother took me roller skating every weekday. Even Sunday after church service at the Champs Roller Dome. For fun, I spent many years speed skating. I started to get serious about roller skating in December 2018! I received my first custom setup from Chris Nelson the Riedell 910 flair in October 2018. My new roller skate setup I ordered featured the Riedell 3200 boot, a Snyder super deluxe lite plate, and a toe stop.

Growing up watching many greats from other cities skate and draw people in. Then seeing people jam skate and do friendly battles inspired me. Skating for me is my life, the other half of my soul! It's my fortune! I spend all my time thinking about skating or watching skating.

I'm currently a sponsored skater for the Enforml Company brand. I started as a brand ambassador, which turned into a Team Enforml sponsorship! This is a new and growing brand of skater clothing and I am honored to represent them.

Ever since taking this path I have a better understanding of how much something so simple can impact hundreds of people! I stick to the middle I'm a 'middle' skater having studied greats like Terminator Tex and clips of the Wizards on Wheels and current videos of other skaters.

If I can advise new skaters, one thing I have to say to the ones starting this journey is to make the most with what you got! Practice and have fun doing it! We're all on the same path some are just ahead of others but in the end, it's all for the love of the art! I get great pleasure by watching young kids skate and have fun, just as I do. Skate not for fame but the love of the art!

Once I complete my time in the military, I plan to hit the skate scene hard and attend as many events as possible. One thing that would make my roll euphoric is if there was a remake of *Skate Music* by Nizm, that jam there is fiyah!!

ABOUT THE AUTHOR:

Hello, my name is Israel Jacob Strong (IsTheWiz), from Louisville, Kentucky. At the time of writing this, I am twenty years old. Neo-soul and rhythm and blues are my favorite genres of music. Currently, I serve as a US Marine—USMC 0311 Infantry Rifleman. I am also a multi-instrumentalist. My passion is skating and once I leave the military, I will spend my time traveling, doing the thing I love most – roller skating.

One quote I like is, "Everything negative - pressure, challenges - is all an opportunity for me to rise." ~ Kobe Bryant

IG@isthewiz
FB: https://www.facebook.com/MEGATRONRULE

HOW IT ALL STARTED FOR ME

Terry Davis

Well, when I look back, my mother was the first person to get me into roller skating. My mom always tried to keep me as busy as possible. She saw that I had too much energy to sit around the house after all my school duties finished for the evening. Mom knew I loved music and loved to dance. She and my dad used to put on that classic, funk, soul, disco, jazz, and rock! Maaan look! Living in my house was like living in a real-life television seventies sitcom with a funk-da-fied soundtrack!

Before I go any further, I want to point out the fact that my parents never skated. My father had picked up some tap dance steps, and incorporated that into his style. He was like a melting pot of funk. Also remember, it was the seventies, so everyone had originality that stood alone. Pop was a smooth-talking, pool-hustling, sharp-dressing, Cadillac driving, pimp hat to the side wearing New Yorker—hailing from Mappsville, Virginia. But he never skated.

My mother was born in Cavern County, North Carolina. Now her is a trivial fact about me. My grandfather was a gentleman named Adolph Parker. Grandfather Adolph had a brother that had a few sons. One of them is Maceo Parker of the one and only James Brown Band. His brother Melvin Parker also played drums for the James Brown band as well. So, when you see me getting extra loose to a James Brown song, now you know why! Not to mention my mom was always singing, dancing, and prancing around the house when cooking or cleaning. Mom and Dad were preparing

So now let's fast forward a bit. Picture it! Sicily, 1955.... Oh sorry, I have seen way too many Golden Girls episodes. The year is 1996. I step foot into The Rink, in Bergenfield New Jersey, for the first time in fifteen years. That is right, I had been there before. This is the rink where my mother brought me to learn how to skate. So, you see this was not my first go around, pun intended. I learned how to go forward, backward, turn, and stop. But I did not learn how to rock. But after spending a week in North Carolina visiting my brother 'Billy D,' aka Bill Davis, and seeing him get loose on the skate floor Empire style—I was ready to attempt to follow in his skate prints and learn roller culture.

Now I'm in the rink yearning to learn! I outgrew my old Chicago skates years ago. So, there I was in brownies. Yes, brownies. I had on straight rental skates! Hey, we all have to start somewhere. Now I hopped on the floor. There are a lot of people on this floor. The music is blasting, the people bumping into me, and the energy is just crazy! It was a Saturday night, and at that time the one and only DJ Mario was on the wheels of steel. Now for those who don't know DJ Mario and DJ Big Bob were the ultimate dynamic music duo of that era, and can still turn a skate jam out today! Mario had caught a groove! He had those turntables moving the crowd. After dodging flying skaters, getting caught in skater pile-ups, and holding on to a few rails I ended up in the middle. Here I saw a display of skills that would forever change my life.

What I saw in the middle of that rink amazed me! Now I am a dancer, always have been and always will be. I have been in a professional paid competition with a lot of dancers. A lot of these dancers I see on TV and film even now. Trust me I am used to a good throw down in the Middle. But this was different. I saw people spinning, doing 360-degree jumps, slides, and using their wheels to slide across the floor like they were on ice! Everyone in the middle was rocking! But I saw one dude do the crazy legs as I have never seen.

I told him, "I need to learn how to skate like that!"

He replied, "It would be next to impossible to become a skater—without first buying a pair of real skates!"

The last thing he stressed to me was coming to learn on Sunday night.

Sunday night was the night! The music was a mix of the new school, old school, and whatever was funky. All the skaters were so cool, but they were mean skaters. The moves went off with such precision. Man, I thought I was in the Olympics or something. All these one-foot spins turns and jumps I thought I would never be able to do what I saw. Then I made my way to the middle. I saw the super smooth brother that suggested I come there on a Sunday in the first place. Right, here is where I started to get in where I fit in, learn things from all the greats of the Sunday night skaters and the Bergenfield Rink.

Now I learned a lot of things from a lot of skaters, but my style is based on two people. These people are the late Chuck Goins senior and his son Chuck junior. Now the people and skaters who were there back then saw Chuck junior do some things that just did not make any physical sense. Chuck has a style that is based on the total manipulation of his wheels. You see, some people pick up and put down their wheels. When they do this, they often use the same muscles as when they walk. Chuck uses the muscles in his legs to move the wheels from one place to the other, making a simple plain movement on skates look dynamic.

By Chuck junior skating at the rink more than his dad, I learned directly from him. Chuck had all these crazy drills he had me do. One drill was to skate around for one or two songs at a time just on my two front wheels. Another was to skate around for one or two songs just on my heels. Then there was one where I was to skate forward on one skate and figure out how to turn my body from front to back while still staying on that one foot. Now to do that last drill that I just mentioned you have to move your front two wheels from the back and move them to the front. This can be noisy, especially for new skaters. But I worked that move until that transition was as smooth as the Moonwalk!

Chuck was quickly surprised at how good I got at these drills, but because of my martial art background constantly working at challenges was second nature to me. I've been training in martial arts for the majority of my life. When I was about nine years old, I became enchanted by watching boxers such as Sugar Ray Leonard and Hector 'Macho' Camacho. Believe it or not, I used to fight a lot in the streets. I became known for the hand skills I worked at, and I was never bullied. I fought a bit too much. Getting expelled from three schools was my record. But that's another story. So, during my last year's 'bid' of a three-year sentence to schools for bad kids, I began to study martial arts.

Sounds kind of backwards, right? But the discipline I learned from practicing martial arts I used in everyday life. So, the more I practiced the crazy and the hard drills, the better I got. When I returned to skating and began to take it seriously, I was a second-degree black belt in Shotokan karate-do. Since then, I have earned the ranks of 5th black belt in Shotokan, a 5th-degree black belt in Macabee Martial Arts School of kung fu, an instructor of the Afro-Brazilian art of Capoeira, and a thirteen-year practitioner of Tracy Kenpo, an accredited original to the Ed Parker system of Kenpo karate.

So now let's fast forward a few months in the future. At this point, I'm learning how to 'crazy legs,' slide, 360, and spin! Shortly after I learn how to skate on a train. Now I'm becoming a force on wheels. I'm also traveling up and the east coast. Now also at this time, there were no big skate parties. So, whenever I went to visit family, I just made sure I brought my skates with me. After about a year and a half, a lot of skaters knew who I was. More importantly, they knew who taught me.

You see I'm very big in giving credit where credit is due. Now, my buddy, Chuck took the most time and showed me the basics of his style. But there were two others as well that were very instrumental in my skating. Andrew 'Dru Boogie,' Smith, and Eddie 'Crazy Eddie' Campos taught me a lot about music and skating. 'Dru Boogie' is a professional DJ that played at 'The Rink' for years. With music credits that are too long to list here. Eddie was a DJ and a professional rollerblader that had a wheel named after him. The dude had his own wheel! That is an incredible accomplishment back then and even now. He also was a former *X-Games* champion. They traveled around the world performing and teaching, but when they came back in town the four of us got down on that skate floor!

Now we were four of a kind and were some of the most influential of our time. Now anyone that knows Chuck realizes that he is a 'super beast' on skates. A lot of people never met him but are doing moves that he created and made famous. Dru Boogie played and created unique mixes on the wheels of steel at the rink, and also created unique mixes that are still emulated in professional mixology competitions all over the world to this day. Eddie, as I said before was a professional rollerblader. He brought the slides he did on the rails and half-pipes to the roller-skating wood! What I love about this is that I see these slides every time I skate! Now please understand, I'm not saying that Eddie is responsible for all the slides in the roller-skating world. But when you see people going forward with the front foot placed on the outside edge and the back on the first two wheels, or any other slide that you would see done in pro-roller blading done on the skate floor, that's Eddie!

Now it was time to come up with a name. Because we were great friends and fans of professional wrestling, we decided to call ourselves 'The Four Horsemen.' One because we four great friends, two because there were four of us, three because we rocked like no others most of the time, and four when we had to perform in a skating event, we shut stuff down like the four horsemen of legend. Those were great times. I miss the Bergenfield Rink. But all good things, as we know, come to an end.

There are certain times in your life that you wish could last forever, but things have to move on. I have had so many great experiences and met so many good people because of skating. Because all of the 'Four Horsemen' were successful in life, we all did not skate together as much in the later years of the rink. Chuck went on to explore lucrative business ventures, Andrew continues to be successful in the music industry, I have a very interesting career in Law, and my brother Eddie went on to still teach, and compete professionally. But sadly, my brother Eddie passed away during a motorcycle accident. Chosen for his skills and talents, Eddie had the opportunity to work on a live-action Disney show that was to run for a couple of years. But God called him home about a year or so into his work there at Disney in Florida. He was my best friend at the time. I was deeply hurt by my brother's loss.

With the passing of my best friend and other various skaters who stopped skating, I really wanted to stop skating. I was at a low point in my skate life. Just a few months before Eddie passed both of my parents passed away. They died one month apart. They fought a great fight against cancer. But after a long hard battle, God thought they fought enough and he brought them home to heaven. So, during these trying times, I was not sure what I was going to do. But thank God for the blessing of my wife, Michelle Moseley-Davis—to keep my spirits up and me skating. My friends Jay and Stephanie Brown created the "Inner Circle" skate family crew. With them, my wife, and a host of other great members being in the crew I was feeling good about skating again.

Around this time, I became a member of the 'Energy in The Middle' skate crew and started learning dynamic skate step routines from one of the best, Harry Gaskin. Harry Gaskin is the founder of 'Energy In The Middle' skate crew and another friend of mine. The skate family can be a powerful thing. Again, I know if it was not for people like Michelle 'OG Lady Jazz,' Stephanie 'Element,' Jay 'Mr. Impossible,' Myra 'Misfit,' Betty 'Crush,' Boop, CJ 'X-sk8,' Khalim 'Nasty Boy,' and the one and only 'Magic,'—I don't know if I how I would have got through some of the times I did. Also, I have to mention Sieon 'The Wise,' and 'Warrior' Duane. I may not see all my skate family all the time, but just know the love is there. I thank you all for reading my intro story to skating.

Skate every day like it's your last, peace love, and roll, and God bless.

ABOUT THE AUTHOR:
Name: Terry C. Davis
Genre: Hip-Hop, soul skating, Breakdancer, deep house, Afro-house, R and B Soul, Rock music, Pop Music, Dancehall, Latin Music
Hometown: Hackensack New Jersey
Affiliation: Inner Circle Skate Crew, Four Horsemen Skate Crew, Energy In The Middle Skate Crew, Macabee Martial Arts International, Knights of Kenpo Karate, Group Capoeira Brasil, Juan Kan Karate-do

About: "Humility is my greatest strength."
I love life, fun, and family.

Facebook: https://www.facebook.com/terry.davis.351756

MY SKATING JOURNEY

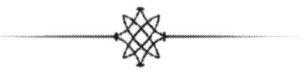

Dr. Joanne Fountaine aka Dove

Started skating when I was very young. I used to wear clip-on skates and skate in the street for hours at a time, with my big boom box blasting! Begging for 'real skates' but, my Mom used to tell me she thought I would throw them into the closet and forget about them like I did everything else. Finally, Mom bought me 'real skates' at age eleven! Those 'real skates' changed my life! I skated every chance I could at the rinks and outside. I remember my Dad getting mad because he had to cart me up to the skating rink and bring me back so often! Eventually, friends joined in and parents took turns driving us to and from the rink. Skating to me was a release. I was very young when I started but, my Mom was also very sick all my life and it scared me. Skating gave me peace. When I was on my skates, I forgot about everything. Skating was in essence my therapy and helped me get through so many things. One of which would end up being the most difficult time of my life—losing my Mom as a teenager. Skating was and still is my go-to when I'm stressed. If you ever heard of 'flow,' skating is my 'flow.' The state of 'flow' is when an individual immerses themselves in something they are doing—and enjoy it to the maximum. When I hit the floor all my worries, stress, and anxiety disappear. It's like I become one with the floor.

As I got older, I acquired friends that skated just like me! The local rink used to call us 'Rink Rats' and we carried that name proudly! We didn't care what music was playing we were there at the rink every chance we got. After my Mom died and I had my firstborn (who is now almost 40) I would bring her to the skating rink in her car seat and she would watch all the skaters as they flew by! The skating rink friends became like extended family and each would take turns holding, feeding, and burping my little girl. By fifteen months, my firstborn was walking, shortly after that, I put skates on her feet —and she still skates to this day!

Graduating from nursing school in 1989, I started a job as a nurse working with dual-diagnosed mentally challenged adults. I decided they needed something fun added to their program and began taking them to the local rink. Eventually, I started renting the rink out once a year for private parties for my clients (on top of taking them to the rinks on prescheduled days) and the staff at the facility all loved it! I enjoyed planning these events and soon found myself occasionally planning events within the general community surrounding skating. Soon, I opened a daycare center and again started planning private events for my clients. Skating always went over big and everyone enjoyed the events I would have.

In around 2001, I visited Ohio. Of course, I went looking for the rinks. When I got into the rinks no matter what rink, everyone was out there jammin'! Everyone was so welcoming and kind. I ended up coming back just to skate frequently. Finally, I decided to move to Ohio as I had never imagined that life could be this fun with this much skating all the time! At the time I moved to a place called Trotwood. Trotwood had this little rink called Hoover. Ms. Juanita, Harry, and Kevin were so kind and welcoming to me. Hoover was the smallest rink I had ever been to in my life but, it would soon become my home rink and one of the best rinks I had ever been to in my life, because of all the love and support at that rink! There were a couple of older guys that would skate on Wednesday mornings. One guy sticks out in my head and I have to give credit to them for teaching me how to elevate my art of skating.

Mr. Joe Bass was a long-time skater and very smooth at it. Mr. Joe may he rest in peace. Mr. Joe used to spend hours teaching me how to dance on my skates and he would watch me as I skated to make sure I was getting the form down correctly.

Mr. Joe would tell me, "I am not going to skate with you until you can go around the rink for a full song without any errors."

I worked on the steps he taught me all the time until I got them down. I will never forget the day Mr. Joe grabbed my hand and told me I did good and was ready! I was so happy! He was so smooth on his skates and to skate with him was an honor! To this day, there is a step I do and when I do it, I say a little thank you in my head to Mr. Joe! Mr. Joe changed my life and for that, I am forever grateful! One day Mr. Joe decided to take me to Castle Skateland in Loveland, Ohio for a National Event. Wow, that floor was huge and the vibe was amazing there! That is what brought me into the national skate scene! Soon, I was traveling everywhere!

As I traveled to different states to skate, I met many new friends from all over the world. Traveling was/is an amazing experience and any skating will tell you, we are all like extended family and are always looking forward to the next time we can meet up on the wood! One friend I met always stood out from the rest, he has been the most honest, trustworthy, respectful, kind, and loyal friend. This man has laughed with me, cried with me, looked out for me, and believed in me. We have had some deeply meaningful conversations—he is a true friend. When I had my first and only National skating event in Minnesota, he came from Philly to support me. When I graduated from my Master's Program, he came to New Jersey to stand by my side and support me. When I was out of town at a skate event and one of the hotels did not follow through with their end of the deal, he was right there by my side making sure they fixed things! Finally, I would like to add because of him introducing me to Amirah I had this and other opportunities that would not have been. So, with this sentiment, I want to thank you Mr. 'Ice'

Clyde McCoy—my dear friend for everything.

Getting back to when I lived in Dayton Ohio, I started having skate parties. The first party I had was a success. I cooked all the food and coordinated the event. It was amazing! And my love for this culture grew even more!

I started having events! Wow, I was having a blast! One day I got a call. My Dad had fallen and broke his hip. Pops was in his 80's at the time. I took a travel nurse job in Minnesota and came back to help him get well.

Once back in Minnesota, I reconnected with my skate friends. I found an elementary school that had a roller-skating class for physical education and thought that was amazing. Knowing the perfect person to call on, I hit up my friend Nate the Skate—and got him booked to come and show off his skill to encourage the students. Nate was a hit! Again, I was out here promoting my passion for skating! I moved back to Ohio once Dad got well, and began traveling with my friends all over the states. Again, Dad got sick, except this time, my brothers called me to come back to care for him. My family and I moved back to Minnesota. Dad got better and lived for four more years.

I started back to skating at the local rinks. At the time there were not a lot of options in Minnesota for adult skating, there were no skate groups really, and not many in-town activities centered around the skating community. I started having an occasional event here and there, started a skating networking group, and more. Soon things were taking off and I started having a late-night adult session. I had never been a DJ but, one thing I knew was music. So, for the next four years, I ran an adult skate session—for which I was the DJ.

The session was a hit! People were coming from surrounding states and supporting the effort. I had a networking group for many years called 'Elite Skaters Connection' and we did community outreach like gathering foodstuffs for the local food banks, helping skaters in need with gifts for children during the holidays, Thanksgiving and Christmas boxes for the holidays—and just about anything. Holding potlucks in my office allowed time for networking and getting to know what each of us did outside of skating. These relationships—built camaraderie—in addition to supporting each other's businesses. I was always into health and wellness so; I would give away free cholesterol screenings and different free tests during our group meetings.

Back at another rink we now had a few adult sessions. My favorite session at Roller Garden was Friday nights. Friday nights were deejayed by "Dollar Bill," a longtime friend. Dollar Bill or Billy (his real name was Baxter but, no one knew it) was unlike any DJ I had ever met. Billy created an ambiance that made us all feel like family. He had a passion for skating, music, and people (Billy could make anyone laugh and smile). The night I came back to the skating rink after being gone many years, I went out on the floor and didn't look up at the DJ booth. Within a few minutes I heard my name over the mic and I knew I was home. After all this time, I was so happy to learn Billy was still there after all these years that had passed while I was living in Ohio. Billy and I caught up for hours. He shared with me that he had become ill and was in and out of the hospital. A short time later, Billy was in the hospital again and everyone seemed concerned that he might not make it. Pulling all the skaters together to go visit him, I got him a tee-shirt that a bunch of skaters signed—and we presented it to him. A bit after Billy's release from the hospital he learned that he was in remission, and he seemed to be improving. Billy was thankful and happy, unfortunately, less than a month later he found out different. Soon, he was having a different conversation with me, one night in particular he told me he needed to talk to me. Billy had a way of always making everyone laugh and smile, but that night was different. I remember Billy putting his arm on my shoulder and looking into my eyes—telling me that he was going to die. I was in denial. Billy told me he didn't know how long he had but—it was coming sooner than later.

 A few months went by and Billy started getting weaker and was in and out of the hospital. One day we were in the DJ booth and he was cracking jokes per usual. Both Billy and I were laughing so hard.

 Billy then said, "When I die, just tell anyone who asks, I'm not in pain anymore."

 I saw a teardrop from his eye and knew he was serious. We hugged and from that day on everything changed. Billy ended up in the hospital and was rapidly dying. He would get out and even with a morphine pump in pain be back up in the DJ booth but, he was losing weight and looking weak. Back in the hospital, Billy never wanted anyone to feel sorry for him—even as he was weak and dying. Billy knew he was actively dying, and went against medical advice leaving the hospital to DJ what would be his last session. I got a call from a friend that told me he was doing the session that night. I went to a trophy shop and had a plaque designed for him highlighting his work in the skate community. That night Billy was weak but he still got out there and did his thing. During his session of a few hundred people, I grabbed the mic, stopped the music, and presented him with the plaque. I saw tears roll down his face and he smiled and gave me a big hug. That night he went home and by morning he passed, my friend was with him all night and she called me to tell me that he looked at that plaque throughout that evening and laid it down next to him. When he died, the plaque she said was laying by his side. Even now as I write this, I am tearing up in knowing that he felt the love we all had for him. I hope he knew those words were heartfelt. I truly believe that plaque helped him to rest easy knowing that his accomplishments will stand in a sacred place of appreciation in our skating community.

I have been known to do pre-thanksgiving events and to share with the skaters how thankful I am for our skating community. A couple of years ago I decided to do something that I felt was long overdue here in Minnesota and that was to acknowledge a few of the long-time skaters for their contributions to our skating community. I gave out trophies to three skaters for their dedication to the skating community. It was a beautiful night, and all that received trophies were well deserved. I had drawings and we acted like kids —playing games like limbo, and having so much fun!

The pandemic created a new need, we lost two skating rinks here in Minnesota in and near the cities. I pulled together a call for action to help our local rinks sustain themselves. I asked the skaters to donate to our local rinks via a Facebook page and the response was amazing! It was awesome to see the community come together. Recently, a lot of younger skaters have started embracing our skate community here in Minnesota therefore, I wanted to connect with them and let them know how amazing and pleasing it is to see them building a beautiful skating community. I travel to their events when I am able and always try to support them. Over the last six months, I created a network of skaters to help me plan an award and recognition dinner/dance event—where I asked the younger skaters to be involved in the planning. My goal is to pass the torch to the younger generation—and impart a sense of purpose with the older and younger crowd. With this effort, hopefully, we can work together as one cohesive unit and keep skating alive in Minnesota. It has been amazing to watch the creativity that is coming from these younger skaters, I feel blessed to still be around and taking part in this amazing time!

As I finish out this chapter, I would like to share a very personal connection related to skating. First, I have been skating almost my entire life.

I think in many ways skating saved my life. We all have things/situations that occur in life and the ways we deal with them. For me, skating has been an emotional, physical, and even spiritual benefit. The friends, connections, and exercise that it brings made a difference for me. See, most of my family have died prematurely to chronic disease and as we know this is a big issue here in the US. My Mom died at the age of 55 of Non-Hodgkin's Lymphoma. When I was a teenager, one of my brothers passed away at forty-one years old due to a massive stroke, while another brother succumbed to a massive heart attack at 49. My other brother had a heart attack at age 49, thankfully he lived.

All my family were obese and had high cholesterol levels. Without skating, I don't think I would be here. My health was traveling down the same path of obesity, high cholesterol, and other detrimental health issues. Not skating caused all of those issues to exacerbate. When I went to get my Masters and Doctorate, I didn't skate as much and became rather sedentary. If I picked up my skating, I would have more energy and feel better. At 57 years old, I still get out and skate a few times a week—this activity and my diet keep me healthy.

After getting out of school I lost about 90lbs, with skating being a big part of my recovery from obesity and near death. Due to the large loss of family and even friends prematurely, I have now dedicated my life to teaching people how to live to their optimal potential—and skating is one way to help make that happen. One goal I have is to share wellness information with our skating family, as so many in our skating community have either had heart issues, stroke, or diabetes or also passed prematurely to these chronic diseases. I hope to share what I have learned and prevent anyone I can from getting sick or dying prematurely and to empower others to live to their highest potential. I have dedicated the rest of my life to the goal stated above. Being that many of my biological family have passed away, our skate family plays a big role in my life, therefore, I can share and empower them with information to help reach their optimal potential in health and wellness, I am always glad to assist. I never want anyone to go through as much premature loss as I and my remaining biological family have faced. My prayer is that I will continue helping as many people live their highest quality of life—for as long as God sees fit. I feel thankful and blessed to continue doing what I love to do—which is helping others as we journey through life together!

My goal in life is to: "Live with intention, integrity, and purpose."

ABOUT THE AUTHOR:
"Live with intention, integrity, and purpose."

I have been skating most of my life. In the skating world, I have coordinated many events, promoted many events, and even deejayed! I know skate music, however; I know only a very small amount about actual deejaying. Amazingly enough, I was able to hold down an adult skate session for over four years, which I thought was pretty successful!

My work life consists of being a Medical Assistant for about thirty-eight years, a phlebotomist for thirty-eight years, and a nurse for thirty-one years. I went back to school almost ten years later in life to learn how to help myself and others reach their optimal potential in health and wellness. I have four degrees, including a Doctorate of Health Education. Skating has been my go-to for as long as I can remember to keep me happy and healthy. I used to say I hope I can skate till I am in my 30's, then 40's, then 50's, now I just say I will skate until the wheels fall off!

Dr. Joanne Fountaine
AKA "Dove"
Owner: Precious Productions
      Ultimate Success Inc.

Facebook: https://www.facebook.com/joanne.fountaine

QUOTE:
Live with intention, integrity and purpose.

ROLLER SKATING ISN'T A JOB

Maurice Jamal Sanders aka Mo "Quadzilla" Sanders

My roller skating life began in the late '70s, during the time of disco. I grew up in the Salishan Projects of Tacoma, WA with my mother and sister Nicky. My dad was an avid skater and as my mom told it, he would occasionally skate from the bars to home if he had too many drinks. My skating journey started with paper grocery bags full of popcorn and a forty-five-minute ride on the public buses with my sister, cousins, and aunt Alberta who would take us to Adams Tacoma Roller Bowl on South Tacoma Way. That was the rink made famous by roller-skating Hall of Fame Coach Skip Peterson and her world champion speed skaters, which included her kids Lynn and Tom Peterson (founder of Hyper Skate Wheels), and future Olympian KC Boutiette among others. We spent as many Fridays and Saturdays as we could there, and if we were lucky a mid-week trip. Back then all the skating we knew about involved speed skating—the main focus of that rink. In the Northwest, you could always tell what rink a skater came from based on how they skated and the skates they had. Speed skaters were from TRB and Pattison's West and Tiffany. Hockey players came from Skateland Olympia, Bremerton, or Burlington, and rhythm/dance skaters came from Skate King in Tacoma, Skoochies in Seattle, and Spinning Wheels in Parkland.

After skating for some years at TRB, they were getting ready to come off the market to new buyers, and we found out that the 'black rink' was now Skate King on the west side of the city, and that's where I got my first taste of what happens—for real—on skates! I watched my dad shuffle around and groove, but it was nothing like seeing the old school skate crews like Black Ice, Palace Crew Rhythm Rollers, and Emerald City Rollers. We saw a skate contest at the rink and it blew my mind. After getting a glimpse of that I wanted to be at the rink 24/7. I met people and made friends that I still have to this day and it all started there. At that age we just did laps, occasionally the races (so we could try and win a free pop or licorice rope), but at Skate King it was all about the rhythm and that's where we learned about footwork, spins, crazy legs, and the rest. They played the music we liked, had people we knew from school and the other projects and it felt like the right place. Nothing made me want to be around skating more than seeing all the moves they did. The early 80's in Tacoma saw the introduction of the LA gang culture and the crack epidemic, and the rink was a big hub of gang activity. Skate King eventually lost its lease and shut down—which led us to find another place to skate. That place was on the outskirts of the city in the rural area of Parkland, which was the 'country' or 'hick town' part of the city and that rink was Spinning Wheels Roller Palace. That became my second home and the real beginning of my 'skate life'.

My cousin Tony and I were inseparable and we LIVED at that rink! No matter how many times I went there, I got excited every time we went. It was Wednesday lady's night, Friday nights, Saturday afternoon and nights, then Sunday adult nights. We watched Jammin' Jerry the DJ, Lenny Stagg, Slick Rick, Sonny, Carlos, and Little Phil. These were THE guys and it got no better than them. They all had different moves and styles and we idolized them all. I watched, asked, learned, and took bits and pieces of what they did to try and create my style, which was hard to do in the 'brownies' aka rental skates. I wouldn't say they took me under their wings, but they let me hang close enough to see and hear what and how to do it. They didn't give me the time of day until I bought some beat-up hand-me-down speed skates from one of the floor guards and it was the first pair of skates I ever owned. The turning point was me getting a job at the rink. Covering for Jammin' Jerry a few times at the rink's mini dance floor during the 'all night skates' helped my cause. After begging my mom, I applied for a position as DJ/floor guard. I became good friends with him and he convinced the owners to give me a shot.

It was 1988 and I was seventeen. That job changed the course of my life and Jerry is one of my two best friends to this very day. Having a reason to be at the rink all the time and getting paid in the process drove me to get better. Learning all that I could about rinks, deejaying, skating, the industry, everything—set me up for future success. I was there at least four days a week, then that transitioned to a manager position. I was the big rink DJ of the area and I had the number one adult night out of any rink. Most Sunday nights we would have four to five hundred people and it was always the 'get down' that you had to be at, even if you didn't skate.

My introduction to inline skating, aka rollerblades, came in '91 from the local sales rep who was trying to convince rinks to rent and sell them. That was another life-changing event, as I tried them and excelled at it. People said you could never 'dance skate' on some rollerblades and I made it my mission to prove them wrong. Jerry and I got into inline speed skating and did a road trip to L.A. for the annual Rollerblade Inline 10K Marathon. It was there that I met Team Rollerblade and the stunt shows that they traveled around the world doing. I came back home to a new thought process and began incorporating my rhythm style into blading, I danced, did launch ramps and halfpipes. Forming a team with some friends I got together—we got sponsored by a local skateboard/snowboard shop that sold inline skates on 35th Avenue. After this success, we would travel and put on stunt shows at the

PNW skate marathons and events.

Part of our trademark for the shows was to do a choreographed dance skating routine followed by skating a launch ramp, jumping over cars, and a VW bus on skates. I acquired my first skate sponsorship with the now-defunct Ultra-Wheels Skates, then went on to be sponsored by local ski company K2 who decided to venture into the inline skate market. I became their first 'pro' sponsored skater. I continued to skate indoors on quads and even did a stint of indoor racing for Pattison's Team Extreme with multiple-time Olympic gold medalist Apolo Anton Ohno. I played around with short-track ice speed skating as a member of the Tacoma Speedskating Club, founded by my friend Jerry. This would be where Olympians KC Boutiette and Apolo Ohno got their starts before going on to world and Olympic championships.

In the summer of '94, I was skating to a local rink for speed skating practice and the rink was at the bottom of a hill. I decided to 'bomb' the hill in a tucked position, little did I know there was a Washington State Patrol Officer clocking cars with a radar gun. He witnessed me passing cars, clocked me, and chased me down the road. The officer clocked me rolling at 53mph and—it was a 35mph zone! I received a ticket for 'reckless endangerment' and a mandatory court appearance. Afterward, we traveled across the inline skate community. I received a call from the organizers of the first-ever ESPN X Games, who extended an invitation for me to compete in the future inline downhill competition the following summer in Rhode Island. My K2 sponsorship furnished my first trip abroad.

I was the brand 'ambassador' and the face of the skate line, so they shipped me off to meet with the European distributors of the brand. I spent six weeks living out of the Netherlands and traveling by train from Amsterdam to France, Luxembourg, Switzerland, Belgium, and Germany. It was trade shows, skate shops, local events, and contests. I had only ever been to California before, and that was only twice, so this was huge. I always took my rhythm skating roots with me and always looked for a place where I could show it. My first time in both Paris and Lausanne, Switzerland, I met a ton of people who were fans of the 'roller disco' as they call it. It was boom boxes and American R&B and Rap music. It was weird and fascinating to me to see non-black people that barely spoke English, embracing, preserving, and displaying the skate culture that I only thought existed at rinks and beaches in the states. I moved to Venice Beach after the X Games to join up with the rest of the top aggressive inline skaters in the US as we traveled competing in the NISS, ASA, and B3 action sports tours. I continued dance skating on my blades as I spent ten hours a day out at Venice Beach with skaters like Terrell, Kyle, Jimmy, Dee, Carl, Jefferey, and a bunch of others.

After a year and a half, I came back to Tacoma to start an inline skate wheel and clothing line under the name Heavy Skate Wheels and Third World. That ran for a few years and at the end of the rollerblading era, I got a call from my friend in L.A. saying they're looking for skaters for a new nationally televised TV show out of Orlando on the TNN cable channel. It was a roller derby show called *RollerJam*. I had watched derby as a kid but never seen one live.

There was nothing else happening for me in Tacoma, so I said, "What the hell!"

I flew down for tryouts, skated, interviewed, and landed a spot on the show! They told me I'd have to live in Florida, so I packed up and went. Got a few roommates, worked a part-time job, practiced 3-4 times a week training with literal legends of old-school roller derby like Little Richard Brown, Buddy Atkinson Jr, Ann Calvello, Ray Robles, Pasty Delgato, and a bunch of others. It was the updated inline skate version of classic banked track roller derby, including all the scripts, theatrics, storylines, and fights. I was a jammer for the Illinois Riot, captained by roller derby legend Richard Brown, and my role was like the Dennis Rodman/bad guy of the show.

My arch-nemesis was the golden boy Jason 'Mac Daddy' McDaniels. The show was wild and lasted about five seasons. We filmed the show and all the games during a three-day weekend and even did a week in Las Vegas at the MGM Grand Hotel.

During the year and a half of living there, I still skated at the rinks like Semoran and United Skates of Tampa. The rink skating never died, even with all of the other skating I was doing, I had to get in one way or another. The ratings of the show were low and it didn't last, so I packed up and went back to Seattle once the show became lost to cancelation. I was working for an old skate friend Attila, who was the cool old white guy that skated at my adult night sessions and sold me my first pair of real 'dance skates.' He had bought a Riedell 297 and Suregrip Classic plate and it was 'too small' so he claimed. (he sold it to me and let me make payments while I worked at the rink). We made a trip to NY (my first time) for a furniture trade show and to meet some clients.

While we there, he told me that I had to skate at Central Park and that I couldn't call myself a real skater if I was in one of the Meccas of skating and didn't roll. That was my first time skating to 80's house music and roller disco. I had no clue what the hell I was doing, but I knew how to ride a beat and I made it work. A few days later I went to the famous Roxy Nightclub, where they had roller skating a few nights a week on their tiny dance floor. I knew of the Roxy from the early '80s and my b-boy days, as that was the spot where Beat Street filmed. My last night in NY and I got to skate at the birthplace/home of roller disco and THAT was Empire Skates in Brooklyn, and that changed everything I thought I knew about skating. I met DJ Big Bob and NY skate legend, Little Mike.

I thought I was doing something on skates with my breaking moves, double kicks, crazy legs, and whatever else, but what Mike did was some next-level shit. The baddest mofos I ever watched skate was Slick Rick Trusty (the smoothest white boy ever) and Lenny Stagg (the most dynamic and energetic), and they were the ones in the PNW with all the outside moves, middle footwork, and everything you could dream of, but when Little Mike skated, it was otherworldly. We didn't skate like that on the west coast, we didn't have the technicality or the creativity. I couldn't even describe it but it changed everything I thought was possible. How he moved, the way he spun, the sliding, turns, edging, the timing and rhythm, the speed and precision. I just couldn't comprehend half the stuff he did.

Once I was back home, with no contractual obligations to be on inline skates anymore—I was back on my quads full time, hitting the rinks. The rink I deejayed at closed, and my adult night session migrated north to Skate King in Kent aka TLC. I picked up where I left off, rejoining all the peeps I used to roll with. It was around this time I found the new flat-track roller derby that started in Austin, TX and made its way up to Seattle. The local league Rat City Roller Girls was getting started and found me thru a mutual friend. They learned that I was a derby skater from television—and that I could teach them how to train and play. This sequence of events started my modern derby scene career.

Around 2004 or 2005 the Roll Bounce movie was being introduced and they had a twenty-five-city competition to find a skate team to perform at the red-carpet premiere of the movie in Hollywood. I put together a small team called 'QuadExpress' with my skate friends Woody and Genny and we entered. We won the Seattle division then went to L.A. and battled it out with the world-famous 'Scooby Brothers,' featured in the Hollywood movie 'Roller Boogie.' The judges were rappers/ actors Lil Bow Wow, Yoyo, and Kool Moe Dee. We managed to win and that got a trip to Chicago for the national finals.

The finals in Chicago had five teams competing for the red-carpet job, which were The Lockwood Boys from Houston, Team Riedell, Philly's Wizards on Wheels, BreakSk8, and us. I had seen lots of good and great skaters, but at the time local skating from the west coast was all I knew. Then I met 'Ice' and Tex from Philly and I wanted to throw my skates in the trash. Again, an east coast style of skating I wasn't accustomed left me floored. Team BreakSk8 eventually won and went on to do the Red-Carpet premier, and later became featured on MTV's America's Best Dance Crew.

I worked for a few years designing wheels for the Matter/Atom Wheels brand then was approached by Riedell to be the brand manager for a new derby wheel line called Heartless. I agreed to take the position on the basis that I could design other products for the skate/derby market. That started my eight-year relationship with Riedell with my brand GRN MNSTR Roller Sports (Green Monster). During that time, I designed the Antik line of skates and accessories including the AR-1 & MG-2 boots, Jet Carbon boot, Reckless Wheels, Morph Wheels, Gumball/Superball toe stops, Moto Bearings, Powerdyne Arius plates, and most notably the Riedell 3200 boot.

After parting ways with Riedell, I moved to Dallas for a new job opportunity. Eventually, that job gave way to me starting my brand of skate wheels, designed specifically for rhythm/style skating called Von Merlin Wheels. Now, I have opened my brick-and-mortar roller skate shop known as Good Foot Skates in the Oak Cliff area of Dallas.

Mo was founding member and skater of the Puget Sound Outcasts men roller derby team (Seattle) for 11 years, 2010 Spring Roll Nationals – 1st Place and MVP Jammer,

2011 MRDA Championship – Silver medal.

Mo played 1 year with Bridgetown Menace (Portland), 2017 MRDA Championship – Silver medal.

Mo has spent the last two years and is a current member of Texas Men's Roller Derby (Dallas), 2019 MRDA Championship –Bronze medal,

Mo was a member of Team USA Men's Roller derby and 3-time MRDWC World Champion 2014 – Gold medal, 2016 – Gold medal, 2018 – Gold medal.

Mo has coached for WFTDA teams Oly Rollers, Rat City Roller Derby, Team Legit and trained hundreds of teams, leagues, and derby conventions all around the world.

Mo was a featured cast member/skater in Disney's movie 'Enchanted' in 2007, and skater and skating stunt consultant for Nike's 'Make'em Miss' commercial featuring Russell Wilson in 2017.

Mo was a competitor in the first ESPN X-Games 1995– downhill inline, later featured in Nintendo video game as Mo 'Johnson', as well as other competitions as the National Inline Skate Series (NISS) 1995-1998, Action Sports Association Pro Tour (ASA) 1995-1998, EPSN B3 (Bikes, Boards, Blades) Competition 1997-1998, Swatch Inline Roller Fest – Lausanne, Switzerland – 1996

Mo was the WSA Jam Skating National Champion – Shuffle skating – 2009

Mo is currently an event coordinator/DJ organizer and skate instructor for the Skate Love Barcelona festival since 2017.

Mo was the founder/designer of Antik Skate Boots brand, boot models AR-1, MG-2, AR-2, Jet Carbon.

Mo was the designer of Gumball/Superball toe stops, Reckless Wheels, Matter Quad wheels, Moto Bearings, Morph Wheels.

Mo was the designer of the Riedell 3200 rhythm boot

Mo owns and designs wheels for Von Merlin Skate Wheels.

Mo currently owns and operates a roller skate shop in Dallas, TX.

ABOUT THE AUTHOR:

Maurice Jamal Sanders, aka Mo, aka Quadzilla L.K., born in (say it with your chest) TACOMA, WA 1971 I have a sister Nicole, nephew Marcquel, a daughter Aris and a son Mekai. I currently live in Dallas, TX.

My dream is to live on the beaches of Venice, CA, or Barcelona just skating around in a just a speedo, with a boom box, fat belly, and live off of tips locals and tourists give me to take pictures with them.

"If you don't expect anything, you'll never be disappointed."

Facebook - @Maurice Jamal Sanders
Instagram - @quadzillalk
Twitter - @quadzillalk
TikTok - @quadzillalk

MEMOIR OF A TREND$ETTA

Bryant Harvey aka Bee1ne

The cul-de-sac was empty except for us. The time that the United States Marine Corps didn't demand from my mother became dedicated to me, and we relished it. The domain of our adventure, this day, would be a section of concrete outside of our house. The straw-covered area reserved for the grass was the only space off-limits to my imagination.

The Onslow County air was warm. The sun's rays sat gently on my mother's cheeks, adding a bit of radiance to her already youthful appearance. I remember the smile on her face as she paused her applause, briefly, to wrestle her wind-tossed hair. It was big and pure and proud. It was June 10th, 1993, and on this day, I turned five years old.

My mother is wholly altruistic and, her gifts are always thoughtful and sometimes prophetic. This gift wasn't any different. They were green and branded Ninja Turtles. The wheels were purple and Raphael, my favorite, adored the ankle of the boot. My first pair of roller skates were a gift for my fifth birthday. My mother and I spent that day together, trying, learning, teaching, and smiling. Of all the things I felt on this day, I didn't fear falling; this is my earliest memory of roller-skating, among others.

Memories fade with time. The memories that I have preserved have a common thread; they are resilient. The events the construct these memories are influential and tethered to roller-skating in some fashion.

As boyish curiosity enveloped my childhood, my interest fractionated; basketball, Mortal Combat, music, Pokémon, and Tony Hawk's 900. The ironic thing about influence is that we don't know what will influence us until it has occurred.

If I were to attribute the title of "Greatest roller-skating influence" to anyone, it would be my aunt LaRita. I come from a family of roller skaters and, my auntie Rita was the coldest Cleveland Freestyle skater I had ever witnessed.

We celebrated my twelfth birthday at United Skates of America; it was Pokémon-themed. That was the first time I watched my auntie skate. I stood attentively in a white FUBU jersey at the entrance of the rink floor. I watched her effortlessly make her way around the rink floor. She would dip, spin, pivot, come back around, and repeat. She had a rhythm when she roller-skated; it captivated me. I spent that day, unimaginatively, attempting to capture the rhythm that my auntie possessed, mimicking her shuffle.

Despite having roller-skaters in my family, I didn't spend copious amounts of time in the roller-skating rink as a child. But when adolescence and its hostilities made their way to my doorstep, I found that I needed an escape. My auntie Rita, mother, and cousin Bo were all adults; 18-30 years older. As a teenager I thought, the things they would do for fun were undoubtedly lame. I was about fifteen years old when that changed.

My mom stored her skates in the laundry room close to the side door. Cleveland winters are brutal, so leaving them in the car was never an option. In the typical fashion of curiosity, it strikes at the most unexpected time. One evening, after school, while waiting for my mom to come home from work, curiosity struck. I decided to slip on my mom's skates. It could have been the conversation that I overheard the night prior between my aunts or the compilation of ghost conversations from years past that centered on Blue Goose Roller Rink. Whatever the influence, I will never forget how I felt when I realized that I could fit the skates. Excited? That was an understatement! I rolled around the kitchen with the rhythm of my auntie or, so I imagined. The fearlessness that I've always seemed to feel when wearing roller-skates straddled my back. I know now that that moment in the kitchen was a sort of initiation. Almost as if the skate God's welcomed me into the fold. I think it was the day that I became a skater.

One Friday morning, just as the first-period school bell rang, I walked into Algebra, found the third desk from the door, and took my seat. Behind me came two of my classmates. One took a desk to my right, and the other took the desk to my left. As they sat, in what seemed like unison, they asked each other:

"Are you going skating?"

In a moment of confusion, I interjected

"You skate? That's what my mom and auntie do."

The girl to my left chuckled and replied

"Yeah, I'm talking about teen-night. You goin'?"

That night I attended my first teen-night at the Rollerdrome. This night I realized that I could be exceptional at skating so, I buried my head in the sand.

Saturday mornings at The Rollerdrome were the sand. Every morning for what seemed like one year, DJ and I, my younger cousin, slipped on our Ridell's, strapped fearlessness to our back, and hit the rink floor.

I eventually returned to teen nights at the Rollerdrome and, on June 17th, 2006, the Trendsetta's or T$C began; I was seventeen years old.

We attended our first national skate jam in Columbus, Ohio, in 2007. IcyHot's second annual skate jam. At its inception, T$C was the youngest group in our skate community. We attended as many skate jams as we could. If it was one thing we knew how to do, it was to create hype around a skate party. At its inception, our youngest member was fourteen years old. We required permission to enter the majority of the skate jams we attended. We traveled all around Ohio and to Chicago, California, Georgia and, Michigan. By 2010, we earned our first nomination for an Adrenalin Award. Our Cleveland Chapter had expanded and, Chapters of T$C were emerging in Cincinnati, Columbus, Akron, Dayton, Chicago, California, Florida, DC/Maryland, and by 2013 T$C became international, adding a Chapter in London, England.

Although we have chapters across the United States with varying skate styles, it is not a requirement for membership, and not all members skate this style, we are prideful about Cleveland Freestyle skating. This style of roller-skating is the root of T$C's skate style. OG skaters like Ty, Smitty and, Darnell were major influences on my development as a skater and of the other Trendsettas. The jumps, spins, shuffle, and pivots are the embodiment of the energy that encompasses Cleveland; the rugged, jollification exhibited on the skate floor is Cleveland. Cleveland is unyielding and taut, and it is auspicious and promising. Most importantly, Cleveland is my home.

As T$C expanded, opportunities were also made available to me. Just as T$C were nominees for and winners of Adrenalin Awards, so am I. In 2010, I won the 'Favorite Inner Circle Male' Adrenalin Award and received a nomination, again in 2011. In 2013, alongside a few of my peers, I skated in the UK Music Festival through a sponsorship with Mahogany Music. One of the best parts of this event was being able to see Stevie Wonder headline the show.

It is imperative to understand that the Trendsettin' Crew is not a skate group. We are all artists-a brotherhood of creatives. Just as my brothers worked on their creative ventures, so did I. I'm an artist. I was an artist before roller-skating and, I'll be one after. What I've been fortunate enough to do is to fuse my love for both art and roller-skating and make money while doing it.

I've been skating, officially, for approximately seventeen years. Within that time, I've attended hundreds of skate jams and met thousands of people. I've had the opportunity to witness some historical events I'll never forget. All that I observed in the skate community, combined with what I learned in a Columbus College of Art and Design classroom, made me ripe for marketing and branding skate parties. So that's what I did.

The first tasks I can recall in the vein of marketing and branding within the skate community are as simple as a t-shirt, flyer, and logo designs for skate groups like the Columbus Originators and Skateology. As time passed, I began to work with various coordinators within the community, branding and marketing events like Independence Roll in Chicago, Illinois, Jive Biscuit in Atlanta, Georgia, and Legends in the Sky in Washington DC, among others.

June 17th, 2016, marked the tenth anniversary of T$C. I've watched many groups come and go. Not only were we still together, but we were still brothers. We had our first, and thus, only independent event in Cleveland in celebration of that monumental anniversary. The magic behind this event is that it occurred on the same weekend same week that the Cleveland Cavaliers brought home a major championship win. This reunion included both former and current members—but forever brothers.

June 17th, 2021, will mark the fifteenth anniversary of T$C. I've always thought that T$C would be forever young. As I near 33 years old, it is important to me that the driving force of T$C, a valuable currency, can remain preserved for all time. In the vein of maintaining its youthfulness, we recruit younger. I've heard several stories from fellow skaters whose youth was literally weaponized against them. Thus, making the rink an unwelcoming place and further decreased the likelihood of joining a skate group. I think that the youth must know that there is no sin in their age. They must also know that the natural process of maturation holds no shame. Regardless of their mistakes, they are worthy. The skate world, collectively, didn't make space for T$C. We, in a way, had to prove that we were valuable. Imagine, as a teenager, feeling the pressure to prove that you love skating just as much as the adults do. I want to be exceedingly clear with the next statement. There were skaters like Wes Giggs, Jokey, Desi Skategrove, Foxy from Dyme Rollers, Ice from Philly, Jst-1-Joy from Cleveland, and CD Man from St. Louis, among others that have become family and never made me feel ashamed of my youthfulness.

I began skating because the hostilities of adolescence made their way to my doorstep but I keep skating for a more complex reason; I love it.

ABOUT THE AUTHOR:

Bryant Harvey is the founder of the Trend$etta brotherhood Est in 2006. He has been skating for over 17 years. He and his brothers were nominated for various Adrenalin awards throughout the years. He won the Adrenalin Award for the favorite Inner Circle Male in 2010. Bryant has skated nationally and internationally attending the UK Music Festival in 2013. He is a graduate of the Columbus College of Art and Design. His designs and style of artistry are second to none. Bryant is a graphic artist, Artist on canvas and surfaces and also specializing in body paint canvases. Bryant is the founder of Dolphin Black Studios. You can find his works at https://www.bee1ne.com/ or at Wild Art Columbus, HomeGoods, Everything but the House, and view his works of arts in cities and towns near you and soon on the internationals stage. He is in one word, a true TREND$ETTA!!

Facebook: https://www.facebook.com/bryant.rivers.12/photos
Instagram: @Bee1ne

QUOTE:
Don't Let anyone take your glory.

HOW SKATING SAVED AND IMPACTED MY LIFE

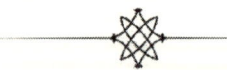

Kevin Williams

I met Laura in September 1980 at Wheels Roller Rink in Windsor, Ontario, Canada. The music was horrible, but her beauty kept me coming back until she finally agreed to a date (eight months later). We saw each other for three years before we married on April 23, 1983. We now have four adult children. At the time of this writing, we have been married thirty-seven years and ten months.

The summer of 1979 was particularly difficult. My five-year high school reunion was imminent. I did not have a job, and with my unemployment checks ending—I was still living at home with my mother and felt like I had not accomplished everything I wanted to since graduation. The embarrassment of going to the reunion came on me strongly—because graduates of our high school had a reputation to excel. Needless to say, I felt hopeless because I did not foresee any new source of income. So, I decided to steal something; anything—to get money.

I conceived this idiotic plan while sitting at the breakfast table. As I pushed back from the table, the phone rang. I started not to answer it; however, internally, I believed I HAD to see who was calling. When I picked up the phone, I began to understand why I had such a strong feeling I must answer.

The voice on the other end sounded nervous.

He said, "Kevin; I don't know if you remember me. I had an urge to call you right away, but it had been so long since we last spoke that I could not remember your number. I prayed that God would tell me your number—and your number came to me. I do not know what is going on in your life, but I do know GOD has a different plan and you have a different path. What is going on in your life? What were you about to do?"

I was shocked and started to cry. I asked him, "...how you could know?"

Benjamin Tucker said, "You already know! You probably remember I am very religious and a firm believer in GOD. HE knows you and is using me to tell you that HE has a plan!"

I told Ben everything, including what I was about to do. In that instant, my life changed. We started to pray and cry together.

While catching up, Ben told me he had planned to go roller skating before he realized he had to call me.

I immediately responded, "Roller skating is for sissies. I would never do that."

He just laughed and said, "You have no idea!"

Ben asked if I was hungry. I told him yes. He offered to come to get me, take me to eat at his expense, and take me to the rink with him.

He said, "We can go to the rink for one hour. I'll pay for your admission. If you do not like it, I will take you back home and return to the rink, pay to get in again, and finish the session."

I do not recall where we ate. However, I remember going to Northland Roller Rink that day. I could not believe so many adults were laughing, talking, and enjoying themselves. The music was on point and the different moves were so entertaining, it was as if a professional skating league paid to put on a show.

Exactly one hour later, Ben came and asked if I was ready to leave.

I said, "NO!"

Then he replied, "Do you still think skating is for sissies?

I said, "No."

Skating was my life from that point onward.

As I mentioned, I met my wife while skating in Canada. Skating has kept me away from criminal activity, from drama—and served my life by introducing me to people whose friendships I will treasure for life. For many years, my life has focused on when I can get to the next session. It has also impacted my health. When I skate regularly, I get all the exercise I need. When I am not skating, I get sick.

I met Jeffrey Owens at a rink. He often spoke of rinks I had never heard of. I had a car, and he knew where each rink was located. We bonded. One day he suggested we skate in Belleville, Michigan. It was a Thursday and you only had to pay $1 to get in. Rollers Skate Park, 19750 Sumter Road, Belleville, MI 48111, is where we went first. It has a beautiful wooden floor. Although it took us a half-hour to get there, it was worth the drive. The session had started, and the music was rocking!!!

The DJ said something I could not make out and he started playing *Function at the Junction* (Mistake 1: Not listening with discernment).

I knew I had to skate to that song as it seemed to be the skate national anthem for Southeast Michigan (Mistake 2: Entering the floor).

As I am skating around the floor in the normal direction, I failed to process something strange was occurring (Mistake 3: Being oblivious to my surroundings).

As I almost completed a second rotation around the floor, I noticed a man skating faster than seemed possible. He turned sideways, put his elbows up and he smashed into a skater about twenty feet from me.

As that skater fell in a heap—he jumped over him and kept coming my way.

What little I can remember includes seeing a myriad of white lights, stars, and blurred vision. Jeff raced over and scooped me up off the floor.

I asked, "What happened?"

He said, "The skater hit you, almost at full speed."

He then chastised me for being on the floor. I wanted to know what hit me, honestly, it felt like a Mack truck on skates—and why the skater did not apologize.

That is when I learned the following critical lesson: If you ever skate in Southeast Michigan and the DJ says...the house is open (or any words similar), get off the floor immediately because it is time for an OPEN HOUSE. For neophytes, it is a simple concept with only two rules.

Concept: you can go in any direction and you can do anything you choose as long as you adhere to two rules.

Rule 1: If you get hit, IT IS YOUR FAULT!

Rule 2: If you get hurt, IT IS YOUR FAULT!

If any questions remain, refer back to Rule 1 and repeat until you understand or you are unconscious!

The principles behind an OPEN HOUSE are not for the meek or easily intimidated. It is equally the most dangerous thing I have ever done on skates and it has been the most rewarding when I needed a thrill. It is extremely dangerous. I have knocked two people out and broken someone's jaw (vertically). During the last incident, my nose broke in three places during that same collision. They take no prisoners in Detroit and you will receive no mercy or sympathy. Now that you are keenly aware of the situation—please travel to Detroit to see it in real-time! You will come away amazed.

Back to sanity and reality!

Five of the most influential people I met while skating: Rockin' Richard Houston, Ice from Philly (I have known this man for decades and STILL do not know his name!!!), Antonio Sturdivant, Cynthia Travis, and Joi Loftin. Here is why.

Rockin' Richard Houston is an extraordinary skater with the ability to perform on skates and cause an entire rink to take notice. Richard was visiting in California and we took him to Sherman Square Roller Rink, 18430 Sherman Square, Reseda, CA 91335. As we all expected, Richard was turning that place out. Suddenly, we heard a commotion coming from the DJ booth. The music stopped and a large man ordered everyone off the floor. Everyone was exiting the floor when the man directed Richard to stay on the floor. As we all looked up in surprise, we learned it was a former football player and actor named Bernie Casey.

Bernie was so impressed with Richard's skills that he wanted to see him skate to a song with no one else on the floor. Yes, Bernie was a skater. So were Janet Jackson, Ed Begley Jr., Michael Warren, Thomas 'Hitman' Hearns, and a lot of other famous people. Perhaps the strangest situation was the fact that Tommy Hearns was skating during his reign as world champion and he would do it on the east side of Detroit. What makes this unique is east side skaters do not care who you are. If you cannot hang, you MUST exit the floor. Otherwise, you will get embarrassed and possibly hurt. The saying on the east side is simple: 'Ride or Die.'

Ice from Philly is an amazing skater, performer and he serves as a mentor to other skaters. You will find him as far away from the drama as a planet will allow. However, he is known to impart wisdom when others need it most. On top of all that, he is a kind and warm man who seeks to learn everything about our history from the other person's perspective and he uses that knowledge to teach and guide others.

If you ever want to see one of the best shows on skates, watch him and Detroit's Reggie Gunn perform simultaneously. They complement each other.

My advice: seek this man out and introduce yourself.

Antonio Sturdivant is a man you may not know by name. BUT... if you have seen the tragedy that befell the Pillsbury Doughboy that was filmed at Skatin' Station II in Canton, Michigan, you will realize you have seen 'Tony.'

Tony (AKA Vant) is one of the best DJs/skaters, I have ever met. He is the man you want to DJ your party. I make this assertion because his blend of music is specific to the crowd he's hired to entertain. He has taught me more about music than any other person. As a guest in our home, he comes bearing gifts, NO DRAMA, and a positive attitude that draws you to him as if he were a long-lost friend.

Tony is so skilled; he can slice through a dense crowd of skaters without touching anyone. Yet, as the Doughboy discovered, it is imperative not to panic when you see him coming. If you do not know Tony, simply look for the man rolling on extremely rare Ultra Crest wheels.

Cynthia is the first lady of skating in Southeast Michigan. Here, I did not include the last name because it's not needed. Everyone in Michigan knows exactly who you are referring to when you say her name. I first became aware of Cynthia when I was with Jeff Owens at a rink we called 'Pontiac.' The rink's actual name is Rolladium Family Fun Center, and it can be found at 4475 Highland Road, Waterford Township, MI 48328. We would go on Sunday nights—which were typically packed. Their DJ was Melvin James and he played 45 rpm records from a turntable. It was an old-school environment. On that night, Melvin played a song that had the whole rink rocking. And, to bring gasoline to that fire, the house was open!

I recall seeing one woman out there hanging with those men. She was smooth, elegant, and graceful. However, she was also a lady who demanded a crowd's full attention while on the floor. I saw her coming full speed the wrong way, skating against the crowd, and then she turned sideways and slide into the corner. My jaw dropped.

I started asking who is that?!? Everyone said, "Cynthia."

I replied, "Cynthia who?"

Everyone replied, "CYNTHIA!"

At that moment, I learned everyone knows who you are talking about when you say her name. Like Ice from Philly, she is a person I will always seek wisdom from. And she is the person most responsible for connecting me with the Queen of the South, and of international skating events—Ms. Joi Loftin.

Joi Loftin is the Queen of the South and the Queen of Skating. Period. She is also wise and one of three women (Laura, Cynthia, and Joi) I trust the most to tell me what I need to hear.

Cynthia encouraged Laura and me to attend Joi's annual skating event held in Atlanta. She connected us with Joi (and John) and encouraged us to create an event in Southern California. That discussion resulted in our 1997 International Roller-Skating Party, held over six days, at multiple rinks. Those events had an attendance of more than 2,000 skaters who arrived from all over the country and overseas.

As I look back on those events, I have regrets and I wish I could turn back the hands of time. If so, I would have been humbler in spirit—and received the insight Joi tried to share with me privately. One of her many attributes is her sharing what you need to hear, in private. I simply wish I had listened. If I had done so, the party would have been even more enjoyable for those that attended.

Through Ben Tucker—my entire life's journey transformed—sending my story arc in a higher direction. Roller skating became the source for improving my health. It also helped me find my wife! Not only that, this culture gave me friendships I will treasure for life. Most of the men at my wedding were skaters. Ben played the organ and Kurt Brown was my best man. From a secular perspective, I assert roller skating saved my life. From a spiritual perspective, roller skating gave me a God-fearing woman and our family.

Each child has a tattoo of a set of skates labeled in a sequence of their birth: I of IV, II of IV, III of IV, and IV of IV.

I love skating and I love how skating has impacted my life.

ABOUT THE AUTHOR:

Decades ago, we established www.rollerskate.net. It will be back online soon. There, you will see lists of popular songs and wheels made for sliding. If you would like to purchase a copy of the videos taken during our skate events or want more information, send me an email (kevin@rollerskate.net).

SKATING IS WHO I AM

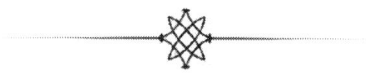

Temptest Hall aka Temptest Nicole

Skating is who I am. It's my escape from the real world. It changed my life.

My name is Temptest Hall aka Temptest Nicole. I'm currently twenty-seven years old, a mother of three—born and raised in Cleveland, Ohio.

When I was a kid, our school would take us on field trips to the rink. During the week in school, we would get coupons for a local skating rink named Zelma George (United Skates). At the time my mom would take us there and my oldest brother would have to hold my hand because I didn't know how to skate. My brother hated it because our wheels would connect causing a fall. As soon as we fell, a floor guard would make us go to the (beginner's/cool-down area) middle circle—which added to my determination in learning how not to fall! That way, my brother's trips to the middle wouldn't have to involve me.

When I was a teenager, Friday nights were 'teen nights' at Zelma. I would go as often as I was able to with my friends—but I couldn't always get rentals because my mom would only send me with the admission money. Having eight other siblings helped my understanding that she did not have the extra money for me sometimes, plus it wouldn't be fair to the rest of my siblings. So, I would just be there hanging out with my friends—which also worked! I was (still am) in love with R&B music—but at the rink—they only allowed backward rink-flow and a couple of skaters on the floor. With my not knowing how to skate in the reverse fashion—I had to sing along and watch. My way of stopping was to skate to the rails or wall to stop myself. We even had a church called the 'The Word Church' that offered a teen night and you got in free if you attended the 'teen church' before the session.

At the end of December 2015, as an adult, I had a coworker who was like my best friend—his name was Jai. He would always mention how he wanted to go skating because he just needed to clear his mind.

One day I said, "Let's go skating! I haven't been since I was a kid—but I know how not to fall."

Jai, I, and a couple of other coworkers went to United Skates of Wickliffe for the adult night which shocked me because I never knew there was such thing as an adult night and that adults still skate constantly as we did when we were teens. While I was in the middle, I was trying to figure out how to skate backward because I never had a chance to learn it as a kid, so I asked Jai to show me.

He showed me how to position my feet and the movements—but then skated away when the song changed saying, "This is my song! I'll be back."

Jai never came back.

We started going to Pla-Mor Roller Rink in Euclid, Ohio the following week to their family sessions. This is where Jai introduced me to two girls named Lexi and Sammi. Both girls skated with me before, so I wouldn't have to skate by myself. Tcfyhey also helped me with learning how to turn around and 'backwards skate.' One day while I was at Pla-Mor, I saw this woman skating so smoothly and effortlessly. She was the first female I hguave seen skating in the moment; she was completely immersed in her own world. Then it clicked, from that moment on—I understood what Jai meant about skating clearing his mind.

I asked Jai if he knew her, he said, "Yeah, that's Jax."

Later that session I saw Jax and her husband.

And in seeing them skate together, I said, "I want to be like them one day."

Eventually, I saw Jax in the middle and I went up to her and said, "I want to learn how to skate like you."

She replied, "Well, the first thing you have to do is get your skates, it'll feel a lot different with a set of your personal skates."

At the time I was starting a new job, so I had to wait for the new skates. In February 2016, Jai took me to "IcyHOT" in Columbus, Ohio at Skate Zone 71. When I tell you I bout lost my mind! It was gone with excitement! There were so many people there from ALL OVER! The music was bumping from outside, we parked far away because the rink parking lot was fully PACKED! The line to get in wrapped around the building. When we finally got inside, the building's situation was no different from the parking lot—IT WAS PACKED! Jai asked me if I wanted to go get some rentals skates and I told him no because I was going to be the only one there that didn't know how to skate. Plus, I had some fear about even trying to get on the floor. So, I watched the whole night from the sidelines. By the end of February, I finally got my pair of skates! To build my skills, I started going skating around five to six times a week.

I've made so many friendships through skating. Many of them are even closer than my own family. I had a skate best friend/sister named India—and our thing was splits! Every session we went to together, we performed the splits. Dating a skater led to a trip to Joi's Sk8-A-Thon in Atlanta, Georgia on Labor Day Weekend 2016. We ended up having a great time, meeting a couple of new people—and skating the nights away. Unfortunately, the short relationship didn't work out, as my skating love interest disappeared. Later on, I found out it was because of an ex and some assorted drama—so I told myself—I wouldn't date any more skaters. In this culture, and locally, I found out many of the people I am cool with—all had some sort of previous relationships. With my being new to the scene, I didn't want to have any drama in my newfound happy place. Things did not get any easier, as dating a 'non-skater' was a headache because they didn't understand how big skating was to me. Assuming I was cheating with someone at the rink always flared up issues—so those relationships never worked out either.

Fast forward to August 2019, we were doing splits at the end of a skate session and a skater recorded me and sent the video.

I posted the video on my social media and to a skate group on Facebook with a caption saying "I'm gonna split until I can't no more, so who's with me?"

India and another skater commented with their split videos. One of the skaters named Kelvin (Pooh) commented with a video of him doing a nutcracker and I replied by saying, "I like my knees."

After this exchange, we became the best of friends. He was in Texas and I was in Ohio, so we did video calls every day since then and would talk about our problems giving each other advice. Pooh mentioned his birthday coming up and that he planned on taking a week off from work. He asked me if I didn't mind him coming up to visit so we could hang out. I agreed, and he booked his flight. I showed him around Cleveland and took him to both of our rinks here—where he ended up knowing a lot of people! As it turns out, Pooh saw people he hadn't seen in forever from traveling to skating parties over the years. A couple of months later, Pooh called India and planned to come to Cleveland to surprise me by asking me to be his girlfriend. India and her boyfriend (now husband) picked Pooh up from the airport, then called my sister Ne'sha to make sure I was home—so she could let him in the house. He walked into my room with flowers and the new *Call of Duty* game that I wanted that just premiered. Needless to say, I accepted and we became official! The next month, I went down to Houston to visit for a date. Pooh gave me a promise ring further declaring his love.

In the summer of 2020 Pooh and January (a JB skater from Chicago but moved to Cleveland at the end of 2019) were talking about how dope it would be if they could get some JB skaters to come to Cleveland and do a JB takeover for a night. So, I suggested that we throw a birthday/welcoming party for Pooh in September since he was moving to Cleveland. We would call it 'Chicago Meets Cleveland.' Upon speaking to Miguel, the owner of Mig's Pla-Mor—he gave us the thumbs up to start planning the event. I made a save-the-date post on social media. January reached out to a couple of skate DJs in Chicago to see who would contact us back first as far as coming to Cleveland to DJ alongside DJ Iceman—who's the home disc jockey for Pla-Mor. We ended up getting a message from DJ T-Rell saying he'll come out and deejay, so we booked him.

One night, I was talking to T-Rell on the phone with Pooh and he was telling me how he couldn't wait to see my pinball split in person and I told him I wanted to see him do a helicopter split in-person. Pooh kept asking me if someone told me to stop in a certain spot—when I do the pinball—would I be able to do it? Every time I told him yes!

September 12, 2020, came, it was now Pooh's birthday and the night of his party. Midnight came so we started roll call and Cleveland went first. After Cleveland, it was Chicago's turn and whenever you go to a skate party that had a Chicago or JB call at the end they do splits and one stops. Everyone out doing their thing we splitting then I hear T-Rell on the mic telling everyone to clear the middle and asked me to come here. T-Rell asked me to do the pinball and land right in front of Pooh so this whole time I'm thinking like okay so y'all are just going to challenge me at the party, bet, let me prove to y'all two that I can do it. So, I come around, pick up some speed and I go for the pinball split and landing right in front of Pooh.

As I turn around to tell him, "I told you so!"

Pooh leaned over and said, "Will you marry me?"

I was lost. Stunned. I replied, "…wait, what?"

I know he jokes around a lot, but then I see the ring in his hand and heard *Let's Get Married* by Jagged Edge playing in the background! Immediately, I started crying—never knowing this whole time I was planning my proposal!

If I can give any advice to any new skaters—it would be to always stay true to yourself and skate for you. There will always be haters in anything you do—but there will also be people who care for and love you as well. Focus on the positive—even when the negativity is louder. Respect others as well as differing skate styles. Learn the history and travel to different rinks. I started posting my first skating videos to try and convince my friends and family to come out and learn how to skate with me. As I got better, my Aunt Michelle would tell me to keep sharing them because she loved to watch them on Facebook. In 2019 she told me not to stop skating. Aunt Michelle told me someone needs to pay me—because I was that good of a skater! Around October 21st, 2020, my mom called and told me that my Auntie had passed away. I made sure that next skate night—I skated as if she was watching. Skating does something to spirit, it's like a natural high with exercise.

Whenever someone comes to me for advice, I'll tell them to try roller skating.

ABOUT THE AUTHOR:

Temptest Hall was born and raised in Cleveland Ohio and is the mother of three beautiful children. She is a entrepreneur producing some of the hottest skate gear to date and is one of the hottest Queens of the skate world.

Facebook: https://www.facebook.com/temptest.hall
Instagram: @Temptestnicole
TicTok: @Temptestnicole

QUOTE:
"Be who you are and say what you feel because those who mind don't matter and those who matter don't mind" - Dr. Seuss

THE ZEN OF SKATING

Sara Messenger aka Sara Embree

My first skating experience, around age six, was kind of like having an introduction to basketball—by receiving a bowling ball to push through heating duct tubing! Well, maybe not quite that bad, but there's nothing less encouraging than trying to roll on a rusty pair of those old strap-on metal-wheeled skates on a rough sidewalk to inspire a lifetime of skate avoidance.

I didn't skate again until I was twelve when one of the little girls in my sixth-grade class held her birthday party at the local rink. That rink was still stuck in the corny organ music phase of American roller rinks, in the white sub-rural community in which I grew up—where I was the token minority of unknown origin.

Of course, I didn't have mad skills that day, but I was rolling comfortably enough within an hour or so that I was soon incorporating the dances of the day into my skating, much to the horror and bewilderment of my more repressed classmates. I had no idea that Black skaters were doing this and a whole lot more all over the country. I thought that it was just me, that I had invented it, that, as usual, I was just weird. I eventually learned that 'weird' was just what some people called it when you had what more knowledgeable people called soul.

It wasn't until I moved to LA and came to Venice Beach that I fell in love with skating, mostly because of the mad skills of the skaters there, and the way one particular skater brought poetry into his every move. I knew I could move like that, and be his partner, and that master of grace with the maddest mad skills, was Jimmy 'Lightning' Stewart, aka the legend, appropriately known as, "MAD."

I didn't approach him, but it was like he read my mind as soon as I had that thought. Although there were hundreds of people there, and he was doing the slow-motion crazy leg, facing another direction in profile to me a few yards away, without ever looking at me, he turned one foot sideways and glided over to me in one fluid motion—stopping inches from where I stood.

Towering over me, he simply said, "What?"

I told him I wanted to skate, and the next thing I knew, the very next day, he was taking me to a skate shop right off the boardwalk, where, in one massive hand, he grabbed me my very first pair of roller skates.

He did take the precaution of asking me how much money I had, and I replied, "I have one hundred and ten dollars to my name."

Which was completely true. I didn't have $110 in cash, with more in the bank, or $110 that day, with a surplus on the way, or $110 in my checking account, but a secret trust fund that I never mentioned like those trust fund kids never do ~ I had $110 to my name, and without even knowing whether I could skate, I spent nearly every penny of my net worth on my first pair of roller skates.

From that moment on, I was out there for hours every day. All I wanted to do was get my bearings, so to speak, well enough that I could move the way I wanted to move, and bring the soulful dance moves to my skating, the same way I once did to cheerleading when I was a cheerleader. Secretly, though I dared not say it, I hoped to get good enough that I could be Mad's skate partner.

So, it was a thrill when he confessed, not long after I first got my balance on those wheels, that he could already see what I secretly knew.

He said, "You're my competition. I hope you're what I think you are, the skating partner I've always been lookin' for."

I knew I had it in me because I was always athletic, always a dancer, and was always passionate about some sport ~ the only girl playing every day on the neighborhood baseball team, the swimmer who did water ballet and got my Junior Lifesaver's certificate years before the age of eligibility, the gymnast and ballplayer that the gym teacher was always trying to get to join the team ~ but I still had a long way to go before I could master all those difficult moves that Mad made look so easy, with his powerful muscles.

As crazy as I was about skating, I was first and foremost a musician, an artist, a quirky creative type, and so was most excited by anything that allowed me to express myself through dance. Water ballet allowed me to dance in the water, cheerleading allowed me to dance in sneakers, tap dancing allowed me to dance while drumming, but nothing was better than dancing on wheels, which is like dancing while flying.

After only a few months of falling in love with skating, I went to Europe for three months with my songwriting partner and had to put those roller dreams on hold. By the end of that trip, I couldn't wait to get back to Venice to resume my skating passion.

It was on our very last day in London that my dreams of skating professionally or in the competition became dashed. I was dancing upstairs in the flat where we were staying with a friend, imagining I was already on my skates in Venice, when he asked me if I could help give a car a jump start. I ran down there enthusiastically, glad to help, feeling good in anticipation of my return to Venice.

I pushed his car down the street a few yards, turned to check the traffic, and started to run across the street, back towards the flat, when a car slammed into me, hitting my forward-thrust knee and running over my foot. I had instinctively looked the wrong way, in a country that drives on the other side of the road.

All I can remember about that night is how it hurt so badly that all I could do is shout, "Oh my god, oh my god, oh my god," over and over, involuntarily, the whole while thinking, "Now all these Brits know I'm a stupid American."

In the trauma of the moment, I didn't have time to disguise my stupid American accent.

Now it hurts like hell, but not even eight broken bones and bone-on-bone knees have stopped me from skating for nearly forty years and loving every excruciating minute of it. Somewhere in between healing from my many injuries and getting old, I got pretty good.

There were things I could never do again, like the sit spins and grapevine moves I was starting to get good at, but there were things I could do on a good wood floor—some of which I can still do, at age sixty-seven—that sometimes got nods from the best skaters.

The highest compliment of all, as Mad himself once heard in the crowd from someone watching me, said "She skates just like a sista."

I wish that there was video footage of me in my prime. Only if at least Mad and my fellow Venice beach skate fam had been there at the big rinks in Baltimore and Chicago (shout out to Henry for rescuing me when I broke my leg at Shake & Bake, and to all the breathtaking skaters at 87th Street, 95th Street, and Rainbow!), when I was really on my game, losing myself in my favorite jam!

I was so into that song the DJ even once stopped to announce, "Look at her gettin' it!" to a rink packed with 300 amazing skaters.

But unfortunately, none of my Venice fams were there during that time, so my best moments on wheels live only in my memory and perhaps in those of a few people who saw something they appreciated that day.

I suppose it's sad that I never got to reach my highest potential as a skater. Moreover, the moment I desired with Mad—that what surely would've been a damn tight skating duo never came to be, but it was never about fame, fortune, or ego for me. It was about the joy, and that was never taken away from me. Skating has been the purest joy in my life, and like all great joy, comes with a certain amount of pain. But I say c'mon with it! It's the only way to live.

I feel sorry for people who don't skate. They don't know what they're missing, and I wish everyone could know that joy, that freedom from our relentlessly troubled minds that comes when you're rollin.'

There's nothing like the sense of freedom and flight you have when you're soaring around the rink, letting the music pulse through your soul and control your muscles as if you were a trusting puppet, in the arms of a gentle puppeteer, and that puppeteer is gravity, centrical force, and grace, and rhythm, and relief, and release—but ultimately all these are just names for God. And it's when you thrust your body against that edge between joy and danger, between flying and falling, when you let go and let gravity hold you, that you can forget all your worldly woes and remember what it's like to be just another precious molecule flying around in Heaven.

Nobody ever taught me how to skate, and goodness knows I've been slow to learn what I know now. Eventually, I realized that skating has been a teacher, not just of the mechanics of skating—but of the mechanics of life.

Over time I realized there were six basic principles of skating, and when I see new skaters, struggling to stay atop their wheels for the first time, I always tell them, if you apply these six principles, you'll be flying in no time:

1. Don't look down.
2. Don't hold onto anyone or anything.
3. Shift your weight from side to side.
4. Bend your knees.
5. Listen to the music, and be a slave to the beat.
6. Skate from your shoulders, keep them level, let them steer you.
7. Lean into it, and throw all your weight into your chosen direction, and most importantly~
8. Skate in the room, not on top of your feet.

Not looking down is about looking where you're going and paying attention to those around you so that you become more aware of others, become a part of the whole, move gracefully in the flow of all the movement around you, and because you're not so self-centered, become less self-conscious in the process.

The Buddhists will tell you that true happiness and enlightenment lies in not forming attachments ~ to people, things, or outcomes. Ultimately, you're on this path alone, you have to find your own path and your own balance, and nowhere is this truer than when skating. Letting go of that wall or that person that you think is holding you up is the first step to finding your stride.

Shifting your weight from side to side, in rhythm to the music, is the constant seesaw of eternity, and like its symbol, the figure eight, creates an endless loop, a pendulum powered by its own movement, each shift providing momentum and relief, so that the weight never remains in one place for more than a second, and we can handle what would otherwise be too heavy a burden. With each shift, we see and feel things from a slightly different perspective, and thus attain a better balance.

Bending, whether it's your knees on the skate floor or the positions you hold in your mind, is the only way you'll move forward ~ in your skating, in your personal growth, and your life. Bending allows you to bounce from one scary moment to the next, and that bounce propels you beyond your fears, into the rhythm that is the heartbeat and lullaby of life.

Letting the music inform your movements is a way of worshipping, of saying in every moment that you can let go of your troubled ego, relinquish control, and trust the Universe to propel you through space. It's also another way of forgetting yourself and being a part of something larger. And it unites you with all those around you as you move to the same rhythm.

When you skate from your shoulders, you skate from your heart, involving your whole body instead of just your feet or legs. Your feet are there to ground you, to connect you to the earth that connects you to everyone on it and are like the rudders on a boat, but they are not the wind that propels you, the helm that steers you, the sails that direct you, nor the mast that balances you. Those things manifest in creation from the whole body working together, directed by the shoulders. Likewise, your life must find balance with the integration of your head, heart, body, and soul, working together, but led by your heart.

To be a great skater or a balanced person, you have to lean decisively into whatever direction you have chosen for yourself. Ain't no half stepping.' Throw your weight behind it with everything you've got, imagine flying, not falling, and trust that whatever happens, it's all good. There's no better teacher than failure, and no true failure other than fear.

If there's one profound lesson that skating has taught me, it's something that I call 'Skating in the Room.' By that, I mean finding your balance, like a tightrope walker, with the longest pole imaginable in your mind. When you balance your shoulders, do it from one end of the room to the other, and in 360 degrees all around you, see yourself as the center of the biggest space you can imagine.

Always be more aware of the skaters around you than you are of yourself. Flow in and out of them as if you are in a dance with infinitely changing choreography. Pay attention to others and celebrate them in every moment, feeling gratitude to be a part of them, a part of the whole room, the whole world, the whole universe that you are skating through. See the good in every one of them, admiring their unique styles, and if you want to truly find your balance, love them, for their willingness to fall, to try, to learn, to risk, and for all their expressions of grace and courage and silliness and audacity.

Love them as they are, for your mutual love of skating, and skate with them, not just among them, to the beat of the same heartbeat, and you will no longer be alone, and perhaps remember, in that little slice of Heaven, who we are and where we belong; moving through space and time together in an infinite universe.

ABOUT THE AUTHOR:

Composer, musician, writer, artist, producer, comic philosopher, and rollerdance fanatic ~ Sara Messenger is a 21st century Renaissance woman who has been obsessed with the arts, sacred geometry, and analyzing the human condition since she was old enough to hold a pencil.

Teaching herself to play piano at age five and guitar at ten, she began composing at seven, put her first band together at eleven, was earning a living as a musician by the time she was fifteen, and touring at nineteen. She released her first album, Tattoos, in 1980 to critical acclaim, making it to heavy rotation on commercial stations including progressive rock and jazz heavies KKGO (Los Angeles), WRVR (New York), WBEE (Chicago), and KFML (Denver), as well as over 100 college and community-sponsored stations nationwide.

She has performed at venues intimate and ginormous all over the States, Europe, and Japan, from legendary clubs like LA's Troubadour, and DC's Cellar Door and Blues Alley, to crowds of 50,000+ at The Washington Monument and activist events from New York to LA. Her 1980 performance at The Michigan Womyn's Music Festival, which she co-produced, had 10,000 audience members and the entire stage crew on their feet in tears. She was more recently featured in Berlin, Germany, at the 2017 HipHop/Bebop Festival.

She has often been called a musician's composer — which explains the list of players who've worked with her just for the love of it, cats who've played with Miles Davis and Stevie Wonder (Munyungo Jackson), Sting, Herbie Hancock, Maxwell, Brian McKnight (Angel Figueroa), Michael Jackson, Babyface, Isley Brothers (Rayford Griffin), guitar masters Grant Geissman, W.G. Snuffy Walden, Marc Antoine, and cats like Doane Perry and Andrew Woolfolk, whose memberships in bands like Earth, Wind & Fire and Jethro Tull are legendary.

A 1993 winner of Chicago's renowned Green Mill Poetry Slam, Sara was also the 1998 featured poet at the 24th anniversary of the Ascension Series at Vertigo Books, curated by Howard University's Professor Ethelbert Miller, where previous features include June Jordon, Alice Walker, and Amiri Baraka.

Her writing has appeared in publications such as *The LA Weekly* and her spoken word performances featured at Hollywood's Poetry in Motion series, The Midnight Special, the LA County Museum of Art, and the historic first trans-continental simulcasts at The Electronic Café.

Sara's focus has always been to use her gifts to inspire, enlighten, and articulate the unsaid, and so much of her work is informed by and dedicated to social issues and spiritual insight. But her great love is roller dancing, which she continues to do as often as possible, even in these dark days of locked-down lives.

Sara performs with her band, *The Brink of Extinction*, at The Rooftop Underground, where she continues to fight—for our right—to parrrtay!!!

THE KING OF SLIDZ

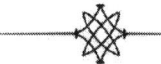

Richard Manning aka The Bird/Sliding Richard

My name is Richard Manning. I'm the owner of an underground roller-skating rink I call 'Rich City' here in Michigan. I fell in love with roller skating back in 1964 at a Sunday afternoon session. I was a four-year-old, shy little boy—but for the love of skating—all of that changed based on the strength of this skating community.

The Rollercade of Toledo Ohio was about eight miles from my house, and every few blocks you would see somebody stop to pick someone up and take them to the rink.

In 1968 the rink, unfortunately, came down to make way for I-75. This event devastated the skating community.

Instead of doing nothing, the community of Lucas County got together to build several outdoor skating rinks all over the city. On top of that, they created a mobile skating unit called the 'skatemobile' that would travel all over the city and was set up for kids to skate at no charge. The program lasted for five summers until they ran out of funds. We skated everywhere after that.

In the early seventies, A young man by the name of Troy opened up a skating rink in the neighborhood. It became known as Swaine Hall—which was across from Swaine Fields shopping center.

It was a wild and rough place, but it was all we had. I don't know what happened over the years but it slowly but surely went out of business. Then came Ohio Skate, after that closed down, next up was Central Arena. I became a teenager traveling with the older skaters to different skating rinks around the Mid-West, as far east as Cleveland, and my westernmost stop was Chicago. When we journeyed south, Atlanta Georgia was the destination.

During my adult years, I've traveled and skated all over the country and in Canada too. I moved to Detroit, Michigan, and lived there for eight years, and at one time—rink officials kicked me out of every skating rink in Detroit for sliding. Looking back, those were some of the best times I had skating and living in the Greater Detroit Metro Area.

I went to a skating party in Flint, Michigan, where I met the love of my life—Peaches. Now she's my wife! She drags me around the floor like a rag doll sometimes on my bad days, and on the good days—we are step for step together. She's my skating partner for life! Our skate friends call her Mama Peaches.

The Art of Sliding

The year was 1966. After a Sunday afternoon session, we would all sit down in the front row of the bleachers and watch a guy rolling on female rental skates—slide from the middle of the floor to the rail and stop with a smile on his face like it was Christmas! He wore those skates because the women's skates always looked newer than the men's skates.

I asked him one day to teach me how to slide and he said to me, "Go down the sideline and go fast as you can—then turn to the side and lean into it—without fighting it."

He gave me his secret on how to slide and slide far! For the past fifty-four years—I still slide using the advice he gave me—and now I pass it on to others.

ABOUT THE AUTHOR:

Richard Manning and his wife Peaches own their own roller rink called Rich City in Michigan. He has been skating for 57 years and has no intention on quitting anytime soon. He is passionate about roller skating and is eager to share his talent to anyone who asks.

Facebook - https://www.facebook.com/richard.manning.779205

QUOTE:
Never say Never!!

MY SK8 LIFE JOURNEY

Lukki Jermaine aka Southern Roll Memphis

As a young black male growing up on the South Side of Chicago, skating has always been a part of my life and has since become a true passion. My brothers, sisters, and I frequented our neighborhood skating rink—Markham Roller Rink on Dixie Highway—three nights a week faithfully. A neighborhood friend by the name of Michael Whitfield taught me how to skate and hold my balance. I started as a speed skater and freestyle skater. Markham Roller Rink also had a club on the inside where we danced to house music if we weren't skating. After we would get tired of hanging out on the club side, we would make our way over to the skate floor to skate for the rest of the night.

Growing up in the Markham Rink allowed me to witness many good, as well as a few bad nights, but in the end, it was all well worth going. The skaters from my neighborhood also attended skating rinks throughout the entire city of Chicago and Gary, IN. Skating wasn't just a hobby—it was essential to me. During the day on Saturdays, my family and friends used to meet up on a street called Ashland Avenue and skate through the neighborhood just for fun. As a kid, there were many nights when I snuck out the window to go to the rink to get my skate on. We even used skating as a means for running errands, like going to the store and picking up food for my mom. I also skated to hustle, delivering newspapers for the Chicago Tribune in the summer and spring seasons.

Mr. Miller, the owner of the Markham Roller Rink, was an influential person in my life, as well as many other lives. He was our City Alderman, my neighbor, and a business owner. He truly understood the importance of giving back to the community and uplifting the younger generation. He oftentimes granted kids free admission into the rink, employed me to cut his grass, and provided a safe environment for the youth to gather and fellowship in our community. The rink was our outlet and our home away from home.

Skating saved my life at times. There were a few incidents that I remember as a teenager that has always stuck with me. There was a time when I had plans to meet a friend at a house party, but I chose to go skating with other friends instead. After leaving the rink, I learned that three people from the neighborhood, unfortunately—got struck by gunfire at that party. I'm glad I chose to go skating that night.

One moment that separated me from skating was a tragic house fire that critically burned my entire family and caused the hurtful loss of my younger brother. I had to go live with my favorite Aunt Nannie but went without seeing my immediate family for months. Aunt Nannie didn't allow skating but made sure I was in church on Sundays. Thankfully later on down the line, reuniting with my parents and siblings in a brand-new home built by the city of Chicago—turned out to be a great blessing!

My grandfather was also severely burned during the housefire. He used to come live with us during the wintertime to work for the Campbell Soup company and provide for my grandmother back home in Mississippi. After his release from the hospital, my grandfather experienced extreme nerve damage from the housefire. My parents would travel from Chicago to the South throughout the year to check on them. Every time we visited Mississippi to check on my grandparents, we stayed in Memphis, Tennessee for the weekend. During our stay, my brothers, sisters and I found a popular hangout called the Crystal Palace Skating Rink in South Memphis.

The Crystal Palace was the most live hangout I had ever seen. When I first stepped foot in the Crystal Palace, it was totally like another skate world. I gained a deep love for Midwest skating because that was all that I knew at that time. However, the Memphis style of skating was so unique that I had to tell my skate friends back home how amazing it was. On every trip that we made to the South, I made sure that we visited the Crystal Palace. Sadly, my grandfather passed away due to his condition caused by the housefire. My parents later decided to stop the long travels throughout the year and relocated to Memphis. After making Memphis our home, I decided to make the Crystal Palace Rink my skate home. It was a smooth transition because I had already gotten to know many people throughout my visits to the Crystal Palace.

I met my first girlfriend at the Crystal Palace and we raised our son as a skate-baby. The more I went to Crystal Palace, the more I became accustomed to how Southern skaters roll. Memphis skating is famous for wall riding. Thirty to forty skaters in one line riding the wall behind each other in unison with a smooth mellow bop was a sight to see. I forced myself to be in that line every time. The Crystal Palace was infamous for its Ladies

Night on Monday Night, Friday Night Late Night, & Sunday Night Live. These were the biggest nights in the city and it was clear that the Crystal Palace had great management. I developed a mad love for Memphis skating. One thing about the Crystal Palace was that the Palace supported the neighborhood. Although closed for business, the Crystal Palace is a landmark today.

The Crystal Palace also had a group of skaters by the name of 'The Rolling Wheels of Memphis' that hosted national parties for years. The Rolling Wheels of Memphis skaters became renowned for their routine style of skating in the middle and around the rink. They were also known to bring skating and unity to the skate floor. Every year around Halloween, the Rolling Wheels of Memphis threw their national party, which brought in different skaters and DJs from many other states. After experiencing several national parties thrown in Memphis, I began to travel to national parties hosted in other states. The first out-of-state national party I attended was 'Skills on Wheels' in St. Louis in 2001. The experience was something out of a skate movie. There were hundreds of skaters from everywhere for three days and three nights. Since then, I've attended that party for nineteen consecutive years.

During my past twenty years of skate traveling, meeting, and building relationships with many skaters was a blessing. It then became more than just going skating to me. I wanted to master the business part of the skate world and host my big weekend. I knew it was not easy to coordinate national parties, so I began to affiliate myself with coordinators like Joy and Trish out of Atlanta, GA, and D-Breez out of Chicago to learn from.

In 2016, the original owner of the Crystal Palace decided to lease the rink out. The person that he leased the rink out to left it the Crystal Palace Rink, but his management skills were not a match to the management skills of the previous owner, by far. The new owners changed some important elements that the original skaters didn't agree with. He got rid of the skate DJ that we had grown accustomed to and hired a club DJ. I knew it was going to be tragic. He removed the pool tables out of the facility and replaced them with white couches as if skaters come to the rink to chill. The real skaters could only take so much of the changes along with admission price increases. Within a few months, he lost the entire skate community as patrons.

Forced to watch this landmark crumble before my very eyes—wounded me deeply! I even set up a meeting with the new owner to try and save it, but

I knew I couldn't do it alone. Nonetheless, I still took a shot at it because of all that built-up passion and talent in this place over the past thirty-plus years. In the end, he didn't have faith in my plan. My own kind! Eventually, with the decrease in business, the Crystal Palace was not able to stay open. Many of my friends just stopped skating altogether and let be a closed chapter of their lives. The remaining few and I started traveling to nearby cities like Little Rock, Nashville, and Huntsville just for a decent adult skate session. It was all good for a while, but I knew something had to change.

    I spent countless nights wondering what I could do to bring adult skating back to Memphis. I just had a gut feeling that I could bring us all back together again. One day, I had the idea to introduce myself to a rink on the other side of town, called East End Skating Center. All I needed was an opportunity. I held a two-hour conversation with the owners of East End and shared my vision. They believed in me without question. One of the reasons why the new Crystal Palace management didn't believe in my vision is because they weren't skaters—they were just leasing it out for the money.

    East End gave me a shot because they lived the skate life along with handling the business. They trusted me with creating a super live adult skate night. With the help of DJ JayTheGreat, we started #SundayNightLive. I formed a promotional team with my dope DJ and we hit the streets running to build something new for all adult skaters in the city. I started posting on Instagram and hitting neighborhoods to let skaters know that we are back. After the word spread, it was a success within months. There was plenty of love and support, along with a lot of envy as well. I promised myself not to feed into anything below my standards but to keep giving the Memphis skate world what they needed—a great skate night. I've even lost many of my skate friends that embraced me when I first came to Memphis for reasons unknown. Honestly, it motivates me to keep elevating. When I proved to myself and East End management that I could bring the local skaters back to the wood with consistent attendance every Sunday, it was time to call them back to the round table.

    In 2016, I had a meeting with the owner of East End and let him know I was ready to host a national party for the upcoming year. He told me to go for it! First, I studied what part of the year would be the best time to have a new national skate party in Memphis. I chose May because of the good weather and the annual 'Memphis in May' festivities—hosted in the city for years! Memphis is best known for our barbecue, so I always choose the same weekend that Memphis in May hosts its World Championship Barbecue Cooking Contest. The next thing was to find the perfect DJs; DJ Soulnificent and DJ Killa B were my first picks because of their widespread support in the skate world.

After hosting my first 'Memphis in May' Southern Roll Sk8 Affair in 2017, I knew I could do even better the next year. I received a lot of positive feedback from the home skaters and out-of-towners. I even had skaters ask me to host skate parties on holidays. From there I started doing Halloween, Valentine's Day, and Thanksgiving skate parties. I used Instagram and Facebook as my platform to promote the parties. I developed a greater passion for skate promotion because I saw how it unified us in the city and beyond. With the help of the best assistant in the world (Ebony), my promotion platform grew. She is a graphic designer and helped me with my flyers and how to optimize my social media insights.

From there, we got into the skate apparel business, coming up with creative designs that no one else was doing. One of our most popular shirts is the Crystal Palace Tee that goes hand-in-hand with our yearly Crystal Palace reunion. This is where many of the CP Skaters who aren't regulars anymore —come and get their roll on with their old skate buddies. As our promotion team grew, we started hosting cookouts and car washes to show our appreciation to the skaters and even began feeding the homeless. Southern Roll Memphis is fondly known for being #BuiltOn1Luv.

Southern Roll is a skating movement for all, no matter the color or creed. With the Almighty's blessings, we are now in our 5th year and still going strong. Despite the COVID pandemic in 2020, we kept the movement rolling. So many of our favorite skate weekends underwent forced cancellation due to government ordinances and the general wellbeing of our public. Even our 4th Annual skate affair was in jeopardy; East End closed down for months and it wasn't looking good. To keep the momentum going, we began attending sessions in other cities whose rinks were open, which eventually became the Southern Roll #Sk8OuttaQuarantineTour.

On the Tour, we hit cities, such as East St. Louis, Little Rock, Dallas, Nashville, Indianapolis, Huntsville, and Birmingham. It got to the point where cities were requesting us to visit them next. Ultimately, our 4th Annual did not happen in May 2020, but the momentum of the Tour helped us with promotion to host it in October 2020. Our 5th Annual 'Memphis in May' Southern Roll Sk8 Affair is May 14-16, 2021 and we're expecting it to be the biggest ever!

I want to say thank you for all of the love and support YOU, the skaters! —have shown in return throughout these last few years. It's what has kept us going! We will forever push for skate unity in our communities.

Mr. Southern Roll #iam ♦♦

ABOUT THE AUTHOR:

Lukki is a roller-skating promoter for Southern Roll in Memphis, Tennessee, where he coordinates events in the skate community and manages a skate apparel line. He is a native of Chicago, Illinois, and relocated to Memphis in 2000. After the move, Lukki opened his professional auto detailing business, Lukki's Auto Spa, which he still owns today. He is a Christian man and a father of two sons. For more information, please follow @southernroll_memphis on Instagram or email southernrollmemphis@gmail.com.

The quote Lukki lives by is, "It is what it is. What it ain't, it'll never be."

THE LIFE OF MSROLLINDIVA

Stacey Davis

"A Fighter for ALL"

I was three years old when my mom placed on my shoes—a pair of Donald Duck skates that had blue wheels, a green plate, white and blue heel, and toe covers with Donald Duck's head on the toe. She held my hand and guided me around the floor during one of our many annual family reunions. Every single-family reunion until I was about ten years old—my entire family ended the reunion day with all of us going skating. Watching my mother and her siblings, John, Crystal, and Gloria, roll in stride in a smooth line one right behind the other with perfect synchronization, I knew at that moment that SKATING was IT for me. I'm a 3rd generation skater. My first pair of REAL Skates I received on my eleventh birthday. Black leather boot, chrome plate, gold wheels, gold toe stop, with yellow gold glitter shoe strings. I wore those skates until my thirty-third birthday. As a teen, (thirteen years old) I was attending adult sessions with my sister, Rae Jean, aka 'Lady Luck.' As long as my homework was not a problem, and my room cleaned— I would wake up for school the next morning knowing I would attend the Wednesday night adult sessions from 9 PM-Midnight.

Once we moved from our small hometown of Hamilton, the true birthplace of Mr. 'More Bounce to the Ounce,' Roger Troutman and Zapp, to the Cincinnati suburbs of Forest Park, Saturday teen nights during the school year and Tuesday nights during the summer months were my must do constant activities. I was the only one in my crew of friends who came to the rink to skate until 11 PM because the DJ would empty the skate floor for the last hour to allow everyone on the floor to dance. And although I was a great dancer as well, skating was my reason to be there and I would get a bit upset to have to stop skating to let everyone else dance. While most people couldn't wait to turn 21 so that they could legally go to the clubs/bars or to buy alcohol, I couldn't wait to turn 21 so I could go skating legitimately on Sunday night. ADULT NIGHT!!

In the late 80s and early '90s, as a new military wife and mom, I now move around the country not only experiencing life away from home but now I'm skating in different cities where I lived temporarily like Newport News, Virginia, and Anchorage, Alaska. Skating during this time for me was fun and therapeutic and made my pregnancies easy.

I skated pregnant with my first two sons each time until I was seven or eight months pregnant—only stopping when I no longer had any cute clothes to fit. As soon as I could return to the rink after giving birth to my first two sons, I was there. With my final pregnancy, although I skated through most of nine months with my first two sons, my last pregnancy was twins this time around. I stopped skating in my 1st trimester because those two guys were HEAVY! This would be the very first time in my life that I went more than a few months without roller-skating. One week to the day of the birth of my twin sons, I was skating! It felt like I was floating on air—as being off bed rest and back to the rink never felt so good!

Now I have four sons, and I am excited to pass on this family ritual of roller skating. Because I learned at three years old, I made sure that all my sons started at that same age. In the mid to late 1990s, I'm learning for the first time in my life that My Grandfather, John Roscoe Brown, Sr. was not only an educator and business owner, but he was also very instrumental in getting black people in Hamilton their own night to skate during segregation. And that my father, Charlie 'Whip' Davis played baseball in the Negro League with Satchel Paige and Charlie Pride. So now my athleticism and love for skating and sports are making sense to me.

Unfortunately, my marriage to my childhood friend was coming to an end. Skating came to the rescue again. I am now a full-time working, single mom of four growing and active sons.

In 2000, I get my first experience of traveling out of my state for a skate party. Detroit was my first time out of town to skate. The music and skate style were new and different. I sat in awe and total amazement. Even as a skater there are times when I see different styles that I find myself transfixed and in awe of what they are doing.

This experience was after I had the pleasure of witnessing my first national skate party, 'Nati Skate Train Event, in my home town given by Robert 'Showtime' Hunter. Watching Rob, his Mom, Ms. Beverly, and his Aunt Janice put on this event made me want to help in any way possible to keep it going. Skating events are A LOT of WORK. The stress of planning and executing a national event can be unbearable sometimes. You're happy to see the sweat and smiles of all who attend your event. But the hassle, complaints, and rude behavior from the few trouble makers can bring a depressed feeling that can seem unbearable at times. After Ms. Beverly's passing, I promised myself that I would be there to help Rob in any way I could because his event had the potential to be something great. And for about five to six years, we did the event together.

In 2007, Rob stepped down and I did it by myself with a few friends I met along the way who came into town and helped me pull it off. The following year The Dyme Rollers of Columbus came on board to collaborate with me. Our event, The Ohio Skate Explosion was from 2008 – 2010 in Cincinnati, Ohio. It was a great time of traveling the country to promote and having a group of women who each had a special quality and expertise to bring to the table to make the event run smoothly without getting overwhelmed with so many responsibilities placed upon only one person. We were able to see and attack problems head-on and fix them immediately.

Having standards and basic diplomatic guidelines made our event fun. People knew when they came to 'Ohio Skate Explosion' the expectations are set on what behavior was not going to be acceptable. I say that because as the creator of the 'zero-tolerance policy' at that time, we needed rules and guidelines established. At times, several incidents happened at other national skate parties that warranted the need for rules and consequences. I was often seen as being mean. But what I am is direct and to the point. And I believe in what is just and right.

2008 was the year of 'Wonder Woman.' Which is how I becoming nominated and eventually the winner of The Adrenalin Award for 'Favorite Female Skater.' After years of campaigning for all my friends and for my state in all categories available for what I consider a very prestigious award created and made By US For US, I was pleasantly surprised and excited. But the story behind the infamous costume was tragic although the smile in the pictures hid the pain very well. Eleven days before I dawn the infamous costume, I sent out an exciting text to all my skate friends nationwide eager to see them the following weekend at "Rolling in the Carolinas". As soon as I hit send, I received a phone call from my sister, Janice. The call was to inform me that our sister Valerie was gone. Murdered by her husband, in what was later determined to be a murder/suicide situation.

In complete grief and total disbelief, I spent the next ten days in a trance and not able to sleep. Five days after burying Valerie, I mustered up enough nerve to wear the outfit I dared my friends that I would do. I won the costume contest at RITC that year and Adrenalin Awards the next year. I'll be the first to tell you that I am an average skater at best. My passion for it comes because of the feeling I get from actually doing it.

Our Skate event was also nominated as well that year along with my small short-lived skate clothing line, SWS (Sista With Skates) Apparel.

Once I moved away from Cincinnati, it was extremely hard to try and continue this event. So, in 2011, I hosted what would be my final skating event. With no support, that entire weekend was pure hell for me. At one point during the last night of the event, I left the skating rink and drove down the street to just cry like a baby. Skating wasn't able to comfort me through this unbearable pain and depression. The next morning, instead of hanging out with family and friends for the next few days, I jumped in my car and headed back to North Carolina. Six days later my childhood friend, ex-husband, and father of my sons—passed away unexpectedly. Skating, the one thing that got me over pregnancies, divorce, depression, and hard times—wasn't able to get me through this.

Moving to a place like Durham, North Carolina, where my normal routine of skating five times a week, went down to five times a year. Even my sons became affected by the lack of skating we were accustomed to doing. In 2016, after years of a lackluster skate life and after losing my dad, I decided to start back skating. So much so I told a friend of mine that I would start teaching her daughter, who was three at the time, how to skate. I was only able to get two sessions in before I had to stop completely. I had been having constant pain in my feet and shortness of breath for a while. But of course, I thought it was because I was not skating as much as I use to and I just needed to get reconditioned.

In August of 2016, I became hospitalized for a full week. With excruciating joint pain and difficulty breathing—I received a diagnosis of an autoimmune disease called dermatomyositis. The doctors also located a blood clot on my lungs as well. A few months later, in October 2016, I was in the hospital again. This time the diagnosis is an interstitial lung disease, caused by the autoimmune disease. And now I have to breathe with the assistance of oxygen 24/7. So much for skating again, right? Well, don't count me out just yet. Skating is what has me fighting EVERY SINGLE DAY against this disease. My specialty doctors know that my ultimate goal is to get back to skating. Skate videos from the next generation, the birth of my first grandchild, and the beautiful memories I have to share with the friends all across this country that I met over the last 20 years are what keep me going.

And now that my four sons, Ahmad, Malcolm, Rashad, and Malik are full-fledged legal adults, I promised that I would skate with them again.

Therefore, until I become eligible for a lung transplant, I will cherish the wonderful memories from my past as I cheer on the next generation from the sidelines.

ABOUT THE AUTHOR:

Stacey Davis is a 3rd generation skater and the daughter of the late Barbara Adams, a skater, and the late Charlie 'Whip' Davis, a Negro League baseball legend. Mother of four sons and grandmother of one.

Activism is in my DNA. Fighting for what's right and just for all. I've been about Black Lives Matter my entire life.

Skate Coordinator of Ohio Skate Explosion from 2007- 2011.

Adrenalin Award Winner for Favorite Female Skater 2009. 'Wonder Woman.'

Professional Seamstress and Embroiderer

Facebook: https://www.facebook.com/embroiderydivaandqueen

QUOTE:
I can be your best friend or your worst enemy. YOU CHOOSE!

MY SK8 HISTORY

Jim Krummenacker aka Big Jim

My name is Jim Krummenacker and I was born in 1978 in Paris. I still live in the north of Paris.

My first pair of roller skates came to me at the age of six. Since then, I have always had a pair at home. For almost thirty years, my roller skates served me growing up in the streets of Paris—where I played with my twin brother on the block.

Never had the idea to dance with my sk8s until I started hip-hop dance skating.

At the age of eighteen, I discovered hip-hop dance with my childhood friends and my brother. Immediately we became hooked and began to participate in a lot of dance battles.

At the same time, I trained myself in contemporary dance and circus arts. Also, I attended a school of dance and circus school.

Now it's been twenty years that I've been a professional dancer and I live off my passion. I work with a lot of dance companies for whom creating, research, and meaning is important.

2017 was the year that I began to take interest in roller-skating dance. While surfing on YouTube, I discovered a roller event in Detroit, 'The Soul Skate,' one of the most famous events in the USA. I saw hundreds of people in a skating rink, dancing to Hip Hop music.

There was: group dancing, some freestyle in the middle of the rink, some trains, and a lot more. I saw a skater do a roller dance skate freestyle and it blew me away!

I told myself, "Oh My God! It looks like HIP HOP dance on wheels!"

It was love at first sight.

Unfortunately, in France at this time Roller-skating dance community wasn't very big and there are no rinks in France.

I decided that I needed to know the feeling of rinks—so I traveled to New York City for two weeks. I loved what I saw there, and when I came back home, I started practicing in my flat with the help of YouTube tutorials.

Immediately, I felt that I had the potential to be a professional skater.

The fact that I already knew how to skate was a huge bonus. I saw myself improve quickly.

However, I was completely lost because of the different styles of dancing in the US and the equipment used there. Luckily, I reached out to a famous skater, Mister Mo Sander aka QuadZilla and he got back to me! He explained a lot of things about the skating culture in the US. I found this mix of different styles extremely interesting and I wanted to learn all of them!

Following a knee injury, I was away from the dancing stage for about a year. I tore my cross ligament after making an acrobatic jump.

At the end of my rehabilitation, the doctor's cleared me to put on my roller skates again. I could only do movements without any rotation.

Therefore, I practiced walking on the spot with my roller skates like a moonwalk. I loved it and saw myself progress day-by-day and until I had full control of my body. With practice and hard work—I managed to create a slow-motion movement that looked like my skating motions suspended in time.

For my neighbor's comfort, I thought it would be best if I laid down plexiglass, a one-square meter platform, on which I could practice. As soon as I received it—I thought it was so great I had to do a show!

That's how I learned to skate dance on a surface of only one square meter!

Still, I continue training on it.

Afterward, the lockdown time came and my little square meter had taken a lot of meaning. It was my secure space.

I took advantage of this period to train hard and I posted one video per day on Instagram.

As a consequence, my way of skating was adapted to this space constraint. To me, it was a creative constraint that helps me find my style.

Of course, at the end of the lockdown and three months of sk!!ating on one square meter, a huge need to escape grew on me.

With a friend, we began to look for new roller spots throughout Paris. It's at this time that the idea of doing my static walk comes to me again.

I told myself, it would be interesting to do it in places where people walk: like the subway, on a railroad crossing, in front of an elevator, even on the roof of a truck. I was looking for spots with the notion of movement.

Everybody is free to give their interpretation of this man who is blocking —but still tries to move forward without succeeding. For me, I see a way to show expression—and roller-skating becomes a form of street art.

My dream would be to travel to the United States and visit as many rinks as possible. Discovering all of the different styles, meeting a lot of skaters to network, and learning about the history of these different movements—are my goals.

Once again, it will make me think of the Hip Hop Culture—where we find different styles like break dance, popping, locking, and house dance.

For roller-skating, it's the same; we have the jamskate, the JB style, the slow walk, and many others with their great history.

But they both share this relationship with Hip Hop music.

It's been more than twenty years since I became a professional dancer. My discovery of roller-skating three years ago—brought me back to my beginnings. Now I have rekindled the pleasures of discovery and training once again.

It's incredible what's happening today with the skate culture!

I dream skate and I'm on my way!

Thank you for supporting the skate culture and enabling its development and for making it a legacy for the new generation.

LONGUE VIE AU ROLLER

Jim

ABOUT THE AUTHOR:

Jim Krummenacker live in Paris and is an avid roller skater. He discovered hip-hop dance at a young age and perfected his craft. He is now a professional dancer in and around Paris. He has incorporated his love of dance into roller skating. Now he finds unique places all over the country to showcase his talent. Follow Jim on his IG to see more of his talent.

Instagram: @jembigjem

QUOTE:
Long Life in Roller Skating ~ Longue vie au Roller

ROLLIN' UNIFIED READY

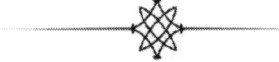

Sam Fonville aka Sam VA Smooth Roller

(In Capt. Kirk's voice)
Skater's log-

Skate date: 0388, these are the voyages into my love for roller-skating and building a legacy (end Capt. Kirk's voice). It was 1988, a good year for my introduction to my first pair of skates. It just seemed like fate, 88, a pair of eights—in which I am destined to skate...yeah, something like that. I remember my very first time in an actual roller skating rink. My godmother, Mama Elaine took me to a rink in the Campostella area of Norfolk, VA, a rink called College Park Skating Center. I have only been in College Park maybe three times in my life. However, the fondest memory I have of being in that place was my godmother showing me how to just walk in the first pair of rental skates I ever put on. It was at that moment I fell in love with skating and wanting to learn everything about it.

Time had passed and my mom and I moved out of Norfolk, VA into Newport News, VA when I was about seven or eight years old. I remember I used to always ask my mom for pair of skates. However, growing up in a single-parent home—at times—would get a bit rough. With her own brand of superpowers, mom would still figure out a way to make things happen. One Christmas Day, my mom surprised me with my first pair of skates outside of the Fisher-Price skates I had when I was three. YES, OH YES, I could smell the fresh new pair of skates in the air. After opening all my gifts my mom came walking up to me with this large square box. Is...is this the day, the day that I've been waiting for (takes a deep breath). Mmm, I think I smell some new skates in the air. So, then she handed me my gift and I begin to tear through the wrapping paper like a dog digging for a bone. YES, MY FIRST PAIR OF SKATES!

(In Scooby-Doo's voice) Wait a minute Raggy these are not the pair of skates I was expecting. Yup, you guessed it. Receiving a pair of rollerblades —which I still was thankful for—but dang mom you had one thing to do and you couldn't...ok, never mind. Nonetheless, I was happy that my feet were in a set of wheels that I could barely stand up in. Those roller blades were killing my ankles and were ripping holes in the inner shin area of my crew socks. I truly had baby deer legs in those roller blades yet, I kept skating in them for a while.

A rink I used to love skating at Peninsula Family Skating Rink with those rollerblades! Each school I attended used to take a group of students skating every Wednesday. I never missed a Wednesday afternoon skate for the world! The skating rink was like a children's club. In the rink, there was food, drinks, arcade games, a pro-shop, candy/toy shop, and the best of them all—THE GIRLS! Being in CLUB MAIN STREET or better yet, MAIN STREET—is what we called it—felt like being in an exclusive club that only the greats came to. Main Street was the scene to be in. While going to Main Street helped me to develop a lot of friendships, relationships, and situationships—heck I was only a kid for skate-sakes. Believe it or not, I got my first kiss at Main Street. My first girlfriend, break-up, and first skate battle was at Main Street.

Remember how I said, "THE GIRLS?" –and to get the girls or at least their attention you had to know how to skate. In my case, I needed to get better at skating and get into the right skates.

On March 27th, 1994, my birthday, I had a big birthday party at Main Street. I was having the time of my life that evening but then... (short pause) ...my mama did that thing again. You know, THE THING with a large square box all nicely wrapped up in gift paper. Could this be the moment of truth? Will my mama redeem herself or will she go down in the book of shame of failed gifts as a parent? Ok, just kidding. My mom handed me the nicely wrapped large square box. Yup, I tore through the wrapping paper like a psycho and opened the box. Could it be, YES, it was a pair of black Riedell Carrera speed skates with the purple wheels and silver dust wheel caps to go with them? Having speed skates during that era was the wave. Everyone I grew up with had a pair of speed skates. I was the happiest kid on the planet for my birthday. I skated in those skates until the wheels fell off of them. No, literally a wheel has fallen off of those skates at least twice within the 7 years I had them. Nonetheless, once those skates were in my possession it helped me build up a sense of confidence, I thought I never would have. Between enhancing my skill set and having a pair of skates I can stand up in. I was highly sure that, 'THE GIRLS,' would be coming my way. I felt like I was unstoppable and the smoothest skater to ever grace Peninsula Family Skating Center. My love for roller-skating grew even stronger.

(Capt. Kirk's voice)
Skater's Log-

Skate Date: 1999, I yearned for something more with roller-skating other than girls and speed I started to crave style and finesse. Then, one day my skates lead me right to the middle of Main Street's floor (end Capt. Kirk's voice). This particular night my mind went on the fritz after all of the talents I witnessed. I approached the center of the floor wondering why a lot of skaters gathered in a circle. There it was the two things I was looking for STYLE and FINESSE. Two guys were tearing up the wood that night in the center of the skate floor. They were doing all sorts of tricks and dance moves from break dancing to stepping. These two men were DOING THE DAMN THANG! Who knew that it would be the night I meet Byrd and Cadillac?

Byrd and Cadillac had this unique style of being FREE on their skates. The style of how they dressed in basketball jerseys and baggy jeans was admiring. Seeing their routines with smooth transitions while skating in unison inspired me to step my game up. However, there was this peculiar thing I noticed about their skates. It was something I have never seen before —they had sneakers attached to their skate plates that formed their skates. WOW, it blew my mind at the age of fifteen. I remember approaching them that night all calm, cool, and collected on the outside. On the inside, I was jumping around like a crazed fan. Anyway, I remember asking them can they teach me something cool on my skates. They taught me a short routine and showed me how to finesse every maneuver gracefully but with power. So, then I asked them what other rinks they skate at and they told me that they skate in Smithfield during an adult session on Sunday nights. Immediately, I felt a bit crushed because I knew I wasn't old enough to go. Who knew that one day I would be surprised about making it to Smithfield Skating rink?

(Capt. Kirk's voice)
Skater's log-

Skate date: some month in 2000, a night I will never forget. Yes, I finally, made it to the Smithfield Skating rink adult night session (end of Capt. Kirk's voice). My Mama Elaine invited me to go skating and at that time I thought we were going to Main Street. Once, I realized we had driven past Main Street I was wondering where we were going. Eventually, Mama Elaine revealed to me that we were going to the Smithfield Skating rink. She and I both knew I still wasn't old enough to go but I didn't ask any questions.

When we arrived and my admission paid—nothing else mattered. I was just thankful. The energy and the music radiating through my body were intense. The crowd was huge and I barely realized there was a skate floor. I had to take a moment to soak it all in before putting on my skates. With my skates were on the real fun began. Seeing all of the different styles of skating was overwhelming. One thing I realized is that Virginia is a big melting pot of various styles of skating. Virginia has no true identity or general style of skating. Skaters were free to embrace any style they wanted. Once again, my love grew stronger for the art of roller skating. On that night I saw Byrd and Cadillac again as expected but this time I saw them skating with two other phenomenal skaters. Who knew that night I would meet the dynamic duo Jit and Diddy?

Jit and Diddy had moves for moves, spins for spins, and footwork for footwork. While they were skating, I noticed one joyous thing they were doing. They were skating with a smile on their face. Even to this day Jit and Diddy skate with a unique rhythm and grace. Their showmanship can be breathtaking at times. Every maneuver was so graceful with impeccable control. I made it my business to personally introduce myself before the night was over. Before I could gain the confidence to do so Byrd and Cadillac put their eyes on me and the next thing, I know I was shaking hands with Jit and Diddy. Ever since that moment, we became history in the making as the Show Out Boyz of Virginia.

For many years we celebrated the art of roller skating by traveling to various places together. Our three-man team grew even stronger once introduced to Travis (Two Stripe), Mike-Mike, and Willy. The team's energy gained a lot of attention through the years and became a well standing and popular force in the adult roller skating community. We formed amazing bonds with many others who shared the same love we have for roller-skating. During our journeys in and out of town, it opened up so many doors for us. Unfortunately, like any good thing they must all come to rest to awaken again someday stronger than ever before. The crew and I are in a time of our lives where our focus is life itself. Between working our careers, marriage, and taking care of our children. It seems like we barely have the time to skate and reconnect on the wood as much as we used to. However, when allowed to pass down knowledge of skate history and becoming a skater in the adult skate realm. We hope to have led other young skaters in the right direction as our predecessors led us. However, were our efforts to spread wisdom taken seriously?

Skater's Log:
Skate date: 2000 and something...

Since the 1960's roller skating wasn't a world unified amongst all races. The division went to a point where the black community had to picket just to skate. In the inspiring words of the Honorable Louis Farrakhan. I am paraphrasing, African-Americans are still at a point in time that our cry is still, "jobs and justice." Why live in a country that claims to be UNITED but divided in so many ways? Eventually, roller-skating had developed into a haven that brought many people together no matter the color of their skin or where they are from, or what set they represent. It took time to get to that kind of dynamic however, skating rinks are still falling, racism is rising and the culture isn't as unified as it used to be...PAY ATTENTION TO THE BACKGROUND! The roller-skating culture is in trouble and leaders of the past and present have to figure out a way to meet in the middle to keep roller-skating alive and thriving. By losing rinks left and right, dealing with gentrification and racial dislocation—these things are continuing to divide us as a human race let alone a roller-skating community.

In 2019 I created my own brand, a movement, and legacy in the making. My brand's name is Rollin' Unified Ready—a movement motivated by the continuous struggles African-Americans endure just to skate. It is also a platform to collaborate and congregate with lovers of the art of roller skating while continuing to UNIFY, EDUCATE, CREATE, SERVE AND SKATE!!! Rollin' Unified Ready stands against inequality, injustice, and immoral acts inside and outside of the roller-skating community.

Through my journey of told and untold stories roller-skating has helped me to build character and confidence. Roller-skating has opened up doors for me to be a part of so many things like showcases, a small commercial, teaching lessons, special guest speakers, special interviews, and currently a chapter in THE EVOLUTION OF SKATING!

Think about it, if the culture of roller skating is properly nourished and treated right—It can become fruitful for all who respect the culture. I don't only skate for the love of it...I skate because it loves me back. Hopefully, someday the Rollin' Unified Ready family and I will encourage change for the better for an ART of endless proportions.

As the good book says in John 15:2, "He cuts off every branch in me that bears no fruit, while every branch that does bear fruit, he prunes so that it will be even more fruitful." (NIV)

We as skaters need to treat the culture of roller-skating the same so, OUR culture can stay alive.

ARE YOU READY?

ABOUT THE AUTHOR:

Sam Fonville lives in Norfolk VA, is married and expecting his first child. He is the Founder of Rollin" Unified Ready and is an Event Organizer for national skate parties under the same banner.

Facebook: https://www.facebook.com/svrolla
Instagram: @rollinunified

QUOTE:
"You can do all things through Christ who strengthen you." - Philippians 4:13

FOR THE LOVE OF ROLLER SKATING

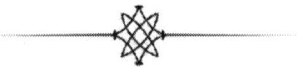

Patricia Bush aka Sweet P

Gosh, where do I begin! So, if you do not know me as Patricia Bush ... You'll know me as Sweet P! I like to look at myself as a Fun-Loving Butterfly with an endless passion for roller skating, dancing, writing, traveling, and music lover! Take a short walk with me, as I introduce you to my busy world!

FOR THE LOVE OF ROLLER-SKATING IS An UNDERSTATEMENT ... Sweet P that's me!

I've always had a fascination with the art of music and how the body reacts to it. This led me to pursue my first dance classes as a little girl. I was the bright and happy young girl that wanted to do every activity under the sun. And that's exactly what my mother provided for me. Every week I would rush to class partaking in Jazz, Theater, and Tap.

The day I learned we had a brand-new roller rink just five blocks down the street from my home in Irvine, California was the day my life changed! My friends and I would gather and literally hang out at the age of seven from opening to close! I was in complete heaven—with the music blasting, folks jamming and everyone happy!

Moving forward, I had the most amazing childhood memories any child could ever ask for! It was until High School my life took a turn for the worst! All the luxuries from being a little girl turned into a fog of hurt and confusion. My pink tutus became replaced with Blue bandanas, Low Riders, guns, and gang affiliations. I'm thankful for the opportunity to write my story because you wouldn't believe some of the things I told you! Sadly, I was the victim of a gunshot wound to the leg by an undisclosed gang on a hot summer night. WRONG PLACE AT THE WRONG TIME HANGING ON THE WRONG CORNER.

It took many months of therapy and I just couldn't believe what was happening to me. I then decided to move to Indiana to be around my closest relatives and leave Los Angeles for a fresh start. This is where my life gets more exciting because I started working at The Indiana State Prison as a Correctional Facility Officer. I also started a family and lived a slow, yet steady life. Eight years later, I decided that was a dangerous career choice, and started a Nursing Career. To cope with the workload and everyday life of a mommy, and studying for my BA, I discovered Zumba, teaching dance classes at the local YMCA, and my lost love—skating. I soon fell back in love with rolling. It's an empowering feeling inspired by a full inner body experience that only skaters would know.

After raising my family, I left the hospital for personal reasons—and was determined to move back to California in 2013. I decided I wanted to take my passion for skating one step further. I set myself a goal: to instruct, motivate and spread the word, so many more people could discover the benefits of a nice good roll! I also decided to figure out how to start my own Skate Club later named Wood Rydrz. (Founded August 7, 2014).

Wood Rydrz is all about community love, contagious energy, and adding that extra spice to any event. Helping them make these impressive changes is what drives me to be the best CEO and positive influencer I can be for them. I hope to touch as many lives as possible because I can honestly say I have some of the best members who have become a real family in my life. Not to mention, the amazing presidents running their chapters—who free me up so I can focus on building a bigger foundation for all of us to enjoy in the future!

So, I started the club and also started my very own travel business. I felt being an entrepreneur is what I was meant to be in life. I've had several degrees, professional careers but none of them gave me what I was looking for—what my heart desired. So, I decided to go against owing thousands of dollars for school and started my travel business full on! Now, that's a whole book by itself! So, now you know, I am a licensed & certified travel agent. What a BLESSING to have one of your greatest passions as a career! And I didn't stop there: I wanted to make a bigger difference to my skaters' lives, by delivering sexy fishnets. With this in mind, the obvious next step wasn't hard to figure out! I wanted to start my own Lingerie Business too!

So eventually, I expanded my travel business while putting Bossy Butterfly's on a short time out!

Predestinations Travel was growing fast and word spread about my services!

THE COMMITMENT

Predestination Travel is a corporate-based travel business. I book flights, hotels, vacations, cruises, secret locations, groups, private celebrity travel, and destination weddings! I knew in my heart this is was what God sent out for me to do because it gives me great satisfaction from the inside out!

Building a brand that needed to be trusted was a hard commitment and something I was determined to show my family and children. So, I had the skate club, the travel business, and fishnet/lingerie inventory but something was empty! Something didn't seem complete!

So, my ah-ha moment came during my favorite annual birthday vacation ......I created this vacation for all my friends, family, and the skate community! I called it CRUISE CONTROL! So now I had an escape—a place where I can lock in all my dreams and goals while sipping on a cocktail, under the sun. A place where I can write, dance, fellowship, and be me with no judgments!

Shortly after specializing in cruise groups, Carnival Cruise Lines offered me a contract of a lifetime! I took it with pride. They sent me on a free 7-day Caribbean cruise for being one of the top sellers in Los Angeles, California. This is when I decided it was time to resume Bossy Butterflys again and try to implement it into my crazy schedule!

Starting a new management position at the famous World on Wheels, that put all my dreams and goals on the back burner for real this time. I saw it as 'the timing being against me,' I guess.

I would get migraines at the rink trying to squeeze in time for my passion and goals—plus run a rink at the same time. It was one of the most depressing times of my life. But I will say this, working at World on Wheels gave me several once-in-a-lifetime celebrity experiences and current opportunities that I am appreciative of having.

COVID-19- MARCH 15, 2020.

The coronavirus started as a health pandemic, but the outbreak will create long-lasting changes to the way we live and work.

Non-essential businesses and government officials closed down for a time. Federal and state levels—are telling citizens to stay home. Schools are closed, forcing elementary to college students to remain housebound as well. With nearly everyone working and studying at home, online video calls are the go-to method for staying in touch with co-workers and friends. Before newly learned security breaches, Zoom became an overnight household name in video conferencing.

Now that companies recognize that employees can easily work from home, the world is on a pause. My brain can switch roles for a second!

With so much idle time, and time to hear my heart, listen to my vibes, and trust what God initially had for me to do—a light bulb went off one morning in the shower! Now is my chance to create BOSSY BUTTERFLYS in exactly the way I want it to be—from scratch!!!!

Something I know my children will be proud of…

Something I know that will make my mommy feel happy and secure…

Something I know the world will support…

Something my sisters will help me grow 100%...

Something I know my only daughter can be a huge part of…

Something I know my boys will be proud of my accomplishment and say, "That's dope Mom!"

Thank you, Jesus! I opened up my very own Lingerie & Gift Shop BOSSY BUTTERFLYS on July 4th, 2020. And it has been the best decision ever!

BossBabes are women who KNOW that they're the business. In our community no dream is too big or aim too high: we encourage women to be unapologetically ambitious and equip them with the kit to create success for themselves. Butterflies are deep and powerful representations of life. I associate the butterfly with my soul and as a symbol of resurrection. endurance, change, hope, and life.

MY NEW CHAPTER

At the end of the day, I wouldn't take back any of my past mistakes, mishaps, life lessons, or anything that has changed my life forever. One thing for certain, the moment my skates hit the wood—I feel so beautiful, so loved, so pure, so free and unjudged. Skating is my only chance in life to intertwine with the now. Nothing else matters but the beat, the music connection, and the energy my body produces.

WOOD RYDRZ SKATE CLUB- Follow us on IG & YouTube.

PREDESTINATIONS TRAVEL AGENCY-- On Facebook/IG /323.285.2606

CRUISE CONTROLL ANNUAL CARNIVAL CRUISE--- every APRIL. TBA

BOSSY BUTTERFLYS ONLINE BOUTIQUE----

www.bossybutterflys.com

Special thanks go out to God, Jamal Visions, My Mommy, My babies, My Grandma, My Besties, My Sisters, My Best Friends Jeanie, Christine, Anthony Curry, Markeith Thomas, Victoria Sallis, My Wood Rydrz Presidents, My Wood Rydrz, Cruise Controll, Phe, Thunder, Charlie J., 2 M's, Amirah, Bryanne, Cleve, Quest, Jerry Beck, E Missy K, Angie Lenoir, Gary and Socks from the D, Tall, Tiger, Tunisia, Tina Queenz, Kianey, Buffy, Drive-By, My favorite DJs, Rink Owners, Joi, Predestinations Clients, Bossy Butterflys Clients, Tillman Twins, My plugs, brands, a host of celebrities, special skaters, venues, and families that have helped me grow over the years.

Stay tuned for more in 2021 as I start my new life in Atlanta, Georgia!

ABOUT THE AUTHOR:

Patricia Bush is the Founder of Predestinations Travel Agency, Cruise Control, Bossy Buterfly's Online Boutiques and the Wood Rydrz Skate Club. She has the energy of a rocket and a smile to match. When you don't find her on the skate floor you will find her operating one of her businesses like the Boss Babe she is.

WOOD RYDRZ SKATE CLUB- Follow us on IG & YouTube.
PREDESTINATIONS TRAVEL AGENCY-- On Facebook/IG /323.285.2606
CRUISE CONTROLL ANNUAL CARNIVAL CRUISE--- every APRIL. TBA
BOSSY BUTTERFLYS ONLINE BOUTIQUE---- www.bossybutterflys.com

Special thanks go out to God, Jamal Visions, My Mommy, My babies, My Grandma, My Besties, My Sisters, My Best Friends Jeanie, Christine, Anthony Curry, Markeith Thomas, Victoria Sallis, My Wood Rydrz Presidents, My Wood Rydrz, Cruise Controll, Phe, Thunder, Charlie J., 2 M's, Amirah, Bryanne, Cleve, Quest, Jerry Beck, E Missy K, Angie Lenoir, Gary and Socks from the D, Tall, Tiger, Tunisia, Tina Queenz, Kianey, Buffy, Drive-By, My favorite DJs, Rink Owners, Joi, Predestinations Clients, Bossy Butterflys Clients, Tillman Twins, My plugs, brands, a host of celebrities, special skaters, venues, and families that have helped me grow over the years.

Stay tuned for more in 2021 as I start my new life in Atlanta, Georgia!

Facebook: https://www.facebook.com/patricia.bushjackson
Instagram: @sweetpakapattycake

QUOTE:
Forget about the fast lane. If you really want to fly, just harness your power to your passion.

ROLLO'S STORY

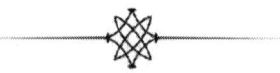

Kenney G. Davis aka Rollo

As a young kid at the age of nine years old my mother and father separated; my Dad decided to take all of his sons—four of us—and move to Cambridge Massachusetts. That is basically where I grew up and my story of roller skating began. Being in a brand-new neighborhood and coming from Washington DC to Cambridge Massachusetts, I didn't know a lot of kids. There was word about a bus that came to our local neighborhood. It turned out to be a long yellow school bus that would pick kids up and take us to the skating rink on Friday nights. There was a benefactor with a private bus wanting to give back to the community. I thought it was a great way to get to know some of the kids in my neighborhood. So faithfully, I would be on that bus every Friday night to go to the skating rink. The rink was known as the Wallex.

Before me roller skating I had a couple of years of ice skating already under my belt so when I put on the roller skates it felt like everything I was not getting from ice skating had finally arrived. Through roller skating I fell in love with it I couldn't wait for the Friday nights to come around.

As I continued to go, some of the kids that were on the bus said, "Hey you're pretty good on those skates."

Although my confidence wasn't that great, I knew I had a lot of admirers. But soon the bus stopped coming, and there was no more Friday night skating. I believe the person that facilitated the trips, Miss Willamina— passed away. I took a year off skating but then a skating store opened up in my neighborhood in Harvard Square. My friends all had bikes and they would always go for bike rides, so I could never go with them because I did not have a bicycle. That store in Harvard Square had a deal renting out roller skates for $5 a day. I would go to the store, rent out the skates and then follow my friends on their bikes. The struggle was real sometimes in keeping up with them—but that made me all the better.

Before I knew it, I had people coming to me asking if I wanted to perform a paid show for them. It only evolved from there; not only did it build my confidence—but it made me want to skate even more. Before I knew it, I was doing shows all around town, so even the Boston Globe had approached me to take on a challenge with the lady with artificial legs. The challenge consisted of me teaching her how to skate, and they would come back in two months to see the results. I accomplished that goal in the article, so when they rolled up—the Boston Globe and their readers were amazed. I was also part of a skate team when I lived in Boston, called the Boston Super Skaters. We met down ast the Hatch Shell almost every day that we had sunshine. I have fond memories of this great team of skaters.

Another proud moment in my life is when there was a huge talent show in Boston at the Strand Theater The Producers were Mr. Maurice Starr and Mr. Tony Rose there were 65 different groups there competing for the prize I came in third place and New Edition came in first that was the launch of their career with Maurice Starr they didn't know what to do with me so they simply gave me the cash and sent me on my way After years of performing in Boston I moved back to the Washington DC area where I was hired at one of the local skating rinks the name of the rink at that time was Crystal Skate.

They hired me as the clown for the skating rink because I was well-versed at doing tricks jumping barrels etc...

One of the workers there said, "Hey you need a clown name!"

He came up with the name Rollo the Clown. That's how I got my nickname, I did the clown for about ten years, then I was offered a contract from Philadelphia to teach at a dance studio came around. After a two-year contract, I moved to Philly. Living in Philly allowed my style to evolve, even more, I met some great skaters out there and we all skated together. People like Ice, Vince, Irv, Tex, Carl, and a few other skaters whose names I can't remember. But I remember us traveling around Philly doing shows all over the place when it came to skating—we were not the ones anyone wanted to play with.

After my two-year contract ended, I stayed in Philly for another two years. After this short stint, I returned to Washington DC. Forming a new skate club called The Mighty Rollers, was my first effort to reboot my skate life in DC. The new group was about twenty-three members strong. With my organizational skills lacking—the group soon died down and folded. Despite this setback, my skating continued to improve just being in the Washington DC culture. Quickly, I joined another skating group call the Anacostia Rollers under the leadership of Miss Betty Dodds.

While I was with the Anacostia rollers, we would do summer shows at

Anacostia Park every summer for years. At one of the shows a young lady came down miss Ann Selman she wanted to audition me for *Showtime At The Apollo Theater*. I auditioned for the Apollo, placed, and won. I ended up appearing three more times at the Apollo, coming in third place at the super Top Dog Show. It was a great experience; one I'll never forget.

Also, for the District of Columbia, I would do all of their parades: The Fourth of July Parade, Cherry Blossom Parade, the Funk Parade, the H Street Festival, and lastly the Martin Luther King Day Parade. Performing at the Lincoln Theater (twice), I had the honor of skating for President Barack Obama. The Presidential Inauguration Committee and The Kennedy Center honored me with being in a short film—which is now enshrined in their archives.

My history with skating goes on and on! I have a forty-year history of entertainment including *America's Got Talent*, also—I just recently booked a movie role being the lead actor in a film called *The Old School Rollers*. I am currently filming my pilot for a syndicated skating show as well. Apple did a story on me calling my skating legacy legendary, and I just recently interviewed with *National Geographic*. There are so many things that I have not mentioned—but I must say skating has taken me to many different places, meeting so many wonderful people—skaters and nonskaters alike. If I had to do it all over again—I wouldn't change a thing.

Roller skating even at age of sixty—is still my life! I currently teach several classes here in the DC area. My Saturday class has over one hundred students and my Sunday session is filled too! God is good, faithful, and rewarding. I hope that my story will encourage you to keep pushing forward towards greatness and encourage you to share your skills and talents with the upcoming generation—passing the torch to leave a legacy.

ABOUT THE AUTHOR:

Kenneth Davis is a professional entertainer and producer with over thirty years of entertainment, performing, and producing experience. He is the founder, CEO, and Creative Director of a new business enterprise, ROLLOWAY PRODUCTIONS, LLC, an entertainment production company incorporated in the District of Columbia in 2014 and located in Oxon Hill, Maryland. The company's purpose is to promote roller skating and inter-generational recreational and entertainment experiences. Its mantra: "Changing the World: Promoting Brotherhood, Health, Joy & Family - Through Roller Skating." He is responsible for overseeing the development and growth of the company's three divisions: Television & Video Production, Live Events Production, and Instructional Programming.

A professional roller-skating performer and instructor, Mr. Davis has been at the forefront of skate-dancing for more than twenty years. He is the founder of "Skillz on Wheels" (2011 - present), an instructional program and performance group for boys & girls, ages 8 - 17. Known as "Rollo," he has presented and performed at numerous festivals, parades, and other live events throughout the metropolitan DC area; is a two-time winner, Best Skate Couple (Adrenalin Awards; 2008 & 2010); a four-time winner of the renowned *Apollo Theater Show Dog* (televised amateur night) competition; and two-time "Third Place" winner of the Apollo's annual Top Show Dog event (finals). From 2009 - 2012 he was the official mascot for the DC RollerGirls derby league, performing at half-time as 'Captain America.' In the early 1990's he made appearances on the *Scott Topper Show*, a popular children's television show based in Philadelphia. One of the most meaningful highlights of his career occurred in the early 1990's when he taught a double amputee how to skate using her prostheses, a story that was filmed and covered by print media.

Facebook: https://www.facebook.com/rollowayproductionsllc
Instagram: @kenny_davis

Quote:
Never make the problem longer than the solution.

THE UK AND BEYOND

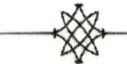

Kris Ward aka Skatemeister

My story started way back when I was between fifteen and sixteen years old—when at school in 1984—I decided to give ice hockey a try. I wasn't a very good player, but I could skate okay and enjoyed it. Playing ice hockey for Brighton in the United Kingdom (UK) for four years led to competing in four tournaments in Holland. I enjoyed every bit of the competition thoroughly and had fun doing what I loved. During that time, I was heavily into music and started a career in deejaying for four more years.

After fifteen years of not skating, I decided to attend the London Street Skate in 2010. This event inspired me to somehow form up a street skate of our own in Brighton. It just so happened that I was skating along the Brighton seafront and met up with a guy named Liam Boraman. I explained my idea of wanting to start our local street skate.

Born and raised in Brighton—I knew the area well. Putting a plan into action, I printed some paper flyers promoting the first street skate. Twelve skaters turned up at our very first event. London Skate had music on theirs, so we had to have the same—if not better. I customized my old DeWalt radio and redesigned the backpack to let the sound blast. This worked fine for a little while, and as the skate grew, so did the sound system. Skaters gave donations to improve the audio equipment. Various skaters and I built a lightweight, radio-linked sound system to take the roller disco to the streets and spread the vibes. My friend Stuart Holt has a unique set of technical skills; he could build and modify any sound system—and did so for us throughout the years. So here we are twelve years later and over seventeen hundred members strong! There are still four of us remaining from the very first year's skate—and what a ride it has been!

Our first skate trip was to Madrid, Spain, which created a spark for three Spanish skate groups to come together—just for our benefit! After that night, the Madrid Friday Night Skate (MFNS) was born. The skate became big enough to require a police escort. We have returned four times for the amazing routes throughout the city, including a nine-mile gentle downhill. After my last trip to Madrid, we received an invite to a roller disco called

Rolling Dance and Burger. I didn't know what to expect from this place, but it was and still is one of the most impressive roller-disco's I have ever seen. After that skate session—dance fever set in on the scene. This made me want to learn more. We went to Sevilla (Spain) and skated on the location of a Star Wars set—and as a Star Wars fan—this was big excitement for me. After this series of events, we heard about SKATE LOVE BARCELONA. Of course, a group of Brighton skaters attended the event along with skaters from all over the UK, Europe, and the USA. Needless to say, what an amazing time we all had!

Back in the UK, we decided to hold our skate dance event. We have found a unique outdoor space by the seafront, under a cliff face. By shining a torch on the cliff face—it givesus a thirty-foot-high silhouette of the skaters on the face of the cliff.

In 2020, despite the pandemic, I had some amazing moments with some great friends in the UK, Europe, and the USA. I also took part in ZOOM sessions with DJ ARSON throughout 2020 (Make Room in That Zoom). We do not have a roller rink in Brighton, only sports halls so skating outside is mainly weather dependent—especially through the pandemic.

One day, I would love to try Central Park NYC, Venice Beach, and Golden Gate Park—if the Skate Gods allow it. My journey in the skate world has been an amazing one so far. Some so many people have been on that journey with me and I want to thank you all from the bottom of my skates.

Skating is not about how good you are—but how much you love to skate. Now Lace 'em up and get out there.

Special thanks go to:
Simon Pert (sound bike)
Asha Kirkby (SKATEFRESH.COM)
Stuart Holt (audio technician)
Stuart Grace (videographer)
Jim Morrow AKA Jimmy �� Blaze
Hjalti Halldorsson (audio technician)
Jake Eley (Locoskates.com)

Many thanks to the Marshalls and everyone else that has contributed to the skate community.

ABOUT THE AUTHOR:

My name is Kris Ward AKA Skatemeister and I am fifty-two years young. So, the Skatemeister is just a bit of fun as I love to skate, Ice or roller, quads, and blades, I am half German so the name went with the profile.

Facebook: https://www.facebook.com/skatemiester
Instagram: @skatemeister

NEW YORK SK8 OF MIND

Mitchell Verley aka Ole' Dirty

My name is Mitchell, from Brooklyn, NY, home of the 1955 World Series Brooklyn Dodgers at Ebbets Field. Also, home of the world-famous, #1 birthplace of roller disco, The Empire Roller Rink. It was 1986 when I started skating at Empire. Located in Crown Heights Brooklyn across the street from Ebbets Field. Today it is now Ebbets Field apartment complex. Back in the mid-1980's Crown Heights was in the midst of the crack epidemic. The area was high in unemployment and had few activities for the youth. As you can imagine, in a poverty-stricken neighborhood crime increased. If you venture out seeking trouble it was easy to find, otherwise, if you mind your business no one would bother you. Once you were inside the rink it was pure joy! Skaters came from all over the state to skate at Empire. The Bronx, Queens, Manhattan, Long Island, and other surrounding areas. People from all over the east coast came to Brooklyn to enjoy Empire as well. Along with premier DJ Big Bob, he plays all types of music hip hop, house, R&B, and reggae. He is amazing and knows what the crowd wants to hear and doesn't disappoint. Once you're inside you can relax and enjoy yourself.

Working as a New York City Traffic Agent, NTCYA, I issued traffic summons to illegally parked vehicles in mid-town Manhattan. A few years earlier, I came out of the military, so I was happy to land a city job. No one prepares you for all the flack you receive while performing your duties. Even when I tried to be fair and warn the person before I wrote their car a summons, it didn't matter. People didn't like being on the receiving end of my summons book. So, trying to be the fair but outspoken Brooklyn guy—I got into a lot of fights. Having piled up so many assault incidents, my coworkers nicknamed the code 10-50 as an 'agent in an assault.' Which in other words translates to—you need help right away!

So, when I call a 10-50, they say, "There goes Mitch again."

I'm not making any light of my job; I do take it seriously.

When I could give a break, I'd say, "A few mins more to move your car but if I come back, I will have to write the violation."

It is stressful every day going to work, and I needed an outlet. One Thursday night a friend invited me to go with him to the rink. I went but I wasn't thinking how much I would enjoy it once inside. The skaters seemed aggressive, and you could tell they didn't like sharing the floor with newbies. Which I didn't get until they started pushing me against the railings surrounded the rink. After I fell, they started to jump over my head like they were going to hit me. I was able to crawl to the side and proceed to go to the smaller rink which most of the newbies were. I decided I wanted to learn, and I wasn't going to stop until I got as good as they were. Even though they were aggressive in skating, they had immense talent, and I wanted to be like them. That night, I went home saying I'll get there one day. The whole time I was at Empire rink I didn't think about work. All I could think of is getting better and going back to Empire roller disco.

Three to five times a week I was at the rink trying to get better, but I didn't have anyone to show or teach me. There were cliques back then and if you knew someone then you were good. Except for my friend who worked at the rink, I didn't know anyone. Until I finally met this older guy, Mike, who used to be in the front of the rink doing little odd jobs. By then I had a car, but you had to get there early to get parking. I spent most of my time driving around. Mike told me to leave my car with him and he would watch it and make sure no one messes with it and I agreed. When I came out, he was sitting inside listening to the radio. I gave him a few dollars and went home until the next time.

One time I asked Mike, "Why don't you go in?"

He told me, "I used to be a regular skater and was good. I belong to the Blue Gorilla skate group. We were well known and respected."

I had no idea Big Mike was a member, "I want to be down with the Blue Gorillas," I said.

He said, "We're not taking any new members but when we do and get enough people, I will let you in."

Now I had something to work for! I asked him about skates and wheels,

"What kind of skates should I get?

He replied, "You should get some Rydell skates and Snyder plates."

I said, "Okay!"

I bought a pair from a skate guru at the rink, and I continued to teach myself. Now I was doing great skating backward but can't stop on a dime or skate forward. I started skating backward so when other skaters came up behind me, they couldn't push me out the way. The more I watched them, the better I got at skating.

It hurt more than I thought when I received the news that Big Mike died. He was a great guy and an even better friend. Mike got me on my way to where I am now! Starting work for the New York City Transit Department—helped take my mind off the loss. As a bus operator for the NYC transit authority in 1988, I felt a huge relief. How bad could it be? You pull into a bus stop, pick people up, take their fares, and they sit down. You go to the next stop and do it again. Boy, I couldn't be more wrong! It was more stressful than any job I ever held, even traffic. I looked so young people would get on the bus and get right off after telling me I should be in school. Kids used to curse me out and threaten me every day. I couldn't believe how the job was changing my personality. I started not caring if they missed the bus or not. The fact was that I had one thing in mind—skating at the rink—so I hung in there! I couldn't wait to get off so I can race home, change, and go skating.

One day I was skating, and I saw this young lady falling. As I reached out to grab her, she somehow took my legs out. Before I could extend my hand out four of my fingers on my left hand went backward and broke. The pain was so intense when I went to the hospital they put a cast on my whole left arm and hand. It destroyed me knowing I couldn't skate anymore for at least a few months. After six grueling months they finally took the cast off and I was able to get back into the rink, I couldn't wait. By then I finally was able to be an all-around skater! I was chatting with DJ Big Bob and he was telling me there was a skate trip coming up in Charlotte, North Carolina. He explained we rent a bus and each person must pay for a round trip bus and hotel fee for the weekend.

"Are you down?" Said DJ Big Bob.

I replied, "Sure, I haven't been to Charlotte, NC and I want to see what this skate trip would be like."

Joining them on the bus going to roll in North Carolina left me full of amazement. All the different skaters from every major city were there. Thousands of skaters from coast to coast. At least 4,000 deep! This is where I saw distinctive styles of skating from, fast backward to g slide, JB, slow walking, stride, and snapping. I fell in love with skating all over again! Since then, I have gone back to Charlotte about ten times. Also traveled to Atlanta for Joi Sk8-A-Thon, Tampa for Soul Roll, and Detroit. I plan to continue attending as many events as possible since they closed Empire Rink due to the violence and complaints. Rumor has it they closed because the owner's husband died, and she didn't want to deal with running the rink anymore. They ended up turning the rink into a storage facility.

A few months go by and there was another rink in New York we could attend. It was in Lynbrook, Long Island called Hot Skates. DJ Big Bob had played there for a while until DJ Arson filled one of his slots. We loved Hot Skates! It had a different vibe and a friendlier atmosphere. When someone fell, everyone stopped to help them up. Ms. Tanya, Dean from Skaterobics held classes before the adult sessions begin. Then we had more people skating and started coming back, it was one big happy family! Each one, teach one, began—and we all loved it!

Years later, the owners of Hot Skates finally admitted they sold the rink. It will soon turn into another storage facility. That leaves one rink standing in New York City! It's also in Long Island called United Skates in Seaford, I'm not complaining. I love skating so much. I finally retired from my job after thirty years as a bus driver. I know if it wasn't for me having somewhere to go and relieve myself of all that stress, I wouldn't last as long as I did. Skating is fun, healthy and it gives you the joy to forget all your troubles. Plus, I met so many peoples from all levels of society. From nurses to doctors, teachers, police officers, and of course, bus operators. We are one big happy family, and we look out for one another.

ABOUT THE AUTHOR:

Mitchell K. Verley was born on the ninth day of December in 1962 and is fifty-eight years young. Mitchell recently retired from NYCTA as a bus operator in 2018! He gave thirty years of civil service to the city of New York. Verley is a former US Army Veteran and NYC traffic enforcement agent. He never married and has no kids. Mitchell is an avid pool player and roller skater. He loves all outdoor activities and has traveled across the globe until the pandemic. Verley hopes to return to school for a bachelor's degree.

Otherwise, has achieved all that he has wanted to do. Mr. Verley does not regret anything he has done in life—for it has made him who he is today. Mitchell is thankful to God and for the love of his family and friends—otherwise, he would not have made it this far. God is good, all the time!

Facebook: https://www.facebook.com/mitchell.verley

QUOTES:

"Enjoy what time we have here on earth. Wishing you all great health and rem love—See you on the wood soon." - Mitch 'Da Legend'

"I still get a kick when people call me that to this day! If they only knew my struggle, well now they will."

"I'm in a New York skate of mind."

"To all my skate family I enjoy what we do, and as we do it, let us fight to keep these rinks open."

BUTTERFLY SEASON: THE BIRTH OF LADY P

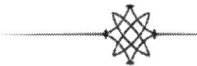

Chaz M. Cunningham Coggins aka DJ Lady P

Formally known as Miss CC-Lady Poetess, now known as DJ Lady P—I was born in Long Beach, CA. Primarily raised in the Inland Empire Region with my Mom, I spent the rest of my time in West LA with my Dad. At the young age of nine years old, I went from being a fully functional outgoing athlete physically and a quick learner in general—to a girl whose life turned upside down with a sudden brain hemorrhage and aneurysm.

Following two brain surgeries in 1995, plus a third unsuccessful surgery—I endured two strokes leaving me with a physical disability on the left side. These events also left me with a learning disability from having a portion of my brain removed. Starting completely over, I had to re-learn everything from the basics and everything else going forward. It came with challenges I never imagined, including learning who I was as a person all over again. However, in losing part of my brain functionality—my artistic side became more enhanced. Later on, in 2018, I decided after receiving unexpected news to have my final brain surgery.

At the time during my marriage, I desired to have children—which would also require me to have brain surgery. The result would be starting over with a different set of challenges. Nonetheless, it would be a beautiful discovery of self—in my own ugly but also amazing way—as I put it. Unfortunately, I did not have the support of my spouse and decided to divorce from an unhealthy environment during the process.

I developed a love for music and poetry overall in Elementary School. Making my mark as a poet in college, I created the name Miss CC-Lady Poetess to stand for the elegance of a 'Lady.' Keeping my initials, a friend gave me the name 'Lady P' when I transitioned into being a DJ. Interestingly, I initially went to college to become a chef, majoring in culinary arts but keeping up started to become both physically & mentally challenging; dealing with subtle discrimination in workplaces from having a disability was stunting my ability to get the career I originally desired. However, my love for the arts, music, and anything dealing with expression or audio grew—as it was my way of coping with life challenges.

By age twenty-six, DJ Lady P (me) decided to invest in the dream of becoming a Professional DJ determined to fulfill my purpose and passion. As one of the first female Radio DJs with *Beyond the Mic Radio Show* on Urban Soul Radio—I made a mark. Making DJ appearances at Soulful Sessions with my former artistic family Jouissance of Expression, So. Cal's Natural Beauty Pageant for Flourishe, RawArtists Pomona Showcase, Da Poetry, and Music Lounge, Xpressions with Holla At Ya Boy Entertainment, Accelerated Radio, All Rhythm Radio, Secret Society Sundays at Nola's with GiftJoy Entertainment, Lemon Flavor Boutique Fashion Show, G&C Media Ent. Events, Rock Boy Fresh Unplugged Concert, The International DJ Cafe, Platinum DJ Cafe, Fireproof the stage play, The Music & Poetry Lounge at The Hilton Hotel, Warrior Women Community, Skate Express, Euphony Restaurant and Lounge, Sevilla's Restaurant, has traveled out of town for other special events, parties, Skate Parties such as ATL's Old School Skate Jam w/ The Super Family, State2State, Sk8fanatics Cali Slide, Skate Lisa's Events, Venice Beach Rollers, East Meets West, Ajaxx, The Sk8Popup, Dallas Sk8 Classic, True Skater Weekend and more. I had the honor of deejaying for some amazing artists—both unsigned and Grammy Award-winning and most importantly community-driven events to give back with the most recent being for the NAACP Pasadena Chapter for their 'Rally for Black Lives.' Specializing in spinning various genres of music works for me, but my favorite type of music to jam to is R&B, 90's, and Old School. I was a DJ on 94.5 The Blaze, Street Madness Radio in Atlanta, and I currently deejay and intern at IMG Radio Network.

Presently traveling all over the country and declared the First Lady of The Platinum DJ Team; as well as MP Productions. You can always expect a personable interaction when working with me; as I am anxious to keep people moving to 'Feel Good Music.'

The quote I use to motivate myself and others in the field of deejaying is that "Music is the sound of Emotion."

Difficulties have shown their face throughout my journey—as such it has been difficult as a Black disabled woman in a male-dominated field, however, it's also been a strengthening and humbling learning experience. It's also made me fight harder for many others like myself and those that are worse off.

You tend to face discrimination at times because of ethnicity, gender, disability, and the more I say this—the better. "It's important to keep going while remembering your purpose through it all."

I believe it's been important to rely on Faith and the tools God has given me to make whatever positive impact we can on the community and the world.

My first experience coming into the skate world stemmed from going to the skating rink with my sister on Friday nights at Skate Express in Chino, Ca. I enjoyed watching everyone and had never really taken in a skate experience like that before outside of getting your regular pair of skates and going outside as a child. It was a different world. Seeing routines, couples skating, tricks—was therapeutic for so many. I wanted to try it, but was timid at first. Especially since spotting this guy who I thought was cute—and didn't want to embarrass myself in front of him knowing my physical limitations. Funny thing is, later on in the night—he approached me as he had been subtly watching my moves. He convinced me to try on some skates and wanted to take me out on the floor. Nervous like a little girl with a schoolboy crush, we did just that—and skated most of the night together, with me getting his number afterward.

I not only fell even more in love with skating but also fell in love with my first boyfriend, as well as my first love. I continued to go to the rink with my sister and meeting up with my boyfriend, and eventually invested in my first pair of skates. Being a tomboy at heart I got personal customs on a pair of skateboard Vans shoes. It was a lot of fun learning and getting out there when I could join the crowd. Primarily the nights that we went were Old School Nights and everyone was friendly, patient, and would look out for me on the floor so I didn't get hurt. At the time DJ Rodney Brewer was the DJ and it was like a family reunion as everyone either knew each other or were related. Chino became home for me. As time progressed, although I enjoyed skating, I felt slightly odd because I could only do so much. However, my love of music coupled with having a good ear; led to hoping that one day I could be a part of that world by deejaying—since I couldn't necessarily do all the routines and tricks. Ironically, I ended up doing just that—and the rest was history.

I started out doing family sessions after having a conversation with Scooby who was the DJ for the Hip Hop night at Skate Express during that time. I applied and had an interview with Joy who gave me a shot as a DJ employee. At first, it was boring for me because I didn't like playing pop and kids' music all day. But I knew I had to start somewhere. So, I did just that and would come up with ideas to present to Jerry the owner when the time was right. Eventually, I earned the ability to have my first adult session; I was incredibly nervous but sitting with my sister Brishae going over song ideas, learning the ins and outs of specials, and talking with close friends turned family—Meghan and Niya—getting their feedback as well, which was key. Learning as much as I could and adding flavor to it, I evolved into the DJ I am now in the skate world by not being afraid to step outside the box, try new things, introduce songs that hadn't gotten airplay before while also giving them music they were familiar with. Initially, it wasn't the most accepted as my approach was different.

Creatively I found a groove and before I knew it, I had unknowingly created a buzz and people began wondering who was this Lady P? My namesake's moniker started getting skaters visiting from other cities—without me knowing until it came to my attention. A solid recommendation by Pete of Skate Fanatics—led to my invitation to DJ the first out-of-town Skate Party in Northern California with 2Raw Skate. With excitement and nerves about the opportunity—I didn't have the best first experience facing challenges I wasn't prepared for. That was her first introduction to regional styles and the history of skate culture. From that point on—I committed to learn as much as I could worldwide—so that when another opportunity came, I would be ready.

Over time with much work put in the skate scene, I became the first West Coast female DJ to deejay in Atlanta, Texas, Arizona, and in 2019 an invitation to be on the itinerary for Soul Skate in Detroit rounded out a big year. Unfortunately, due to the pandemic hitting in 2020, Soul Skate got postponed. However, the humble honor of being a consideration serves as an accomplishment I can always cherish. Skating has developed my persona, Lady P—as a whole—because it teaches you to not only specialize in what you do musically, but as an individual to study, learn, and adapt to everything you encounter. That includes age demographic, regional styles of skating and music, the different cadences and beats that women and men skate to, the history behind tradition, art, DJs that paved the way, and the history of different rinks. Also included is how skating's pivotal role in ending segregation came about—and so much more. Unfortunately, there are skate politics that tend to unfold which can cause discord, competition, and at times can make things discouraging or stressful if you let it. Some of the challenges being a female DJ alone—have their grievances. However, not everyone plays into those things, which has been the good part. In which case I can focus on growing in my gift to be able to share and give back to our community because ultimately skating is therapy for many worldwide. Preserving that safe space is what truly matters most.

I have earned the title of a Professional Traveling DJ specializing in a variety of music. I'm also very big on being a community advocate and activist. In college, I created a group that specialized in all art forms: poetry, singing, musicianship, comedy, rapping, and more. A friend of mine named Michael had a clothing line called, Jouissance of Expression.

I asked Mike what it meant in their poetry class they were talking and he said it meant "Love of Expression" in French.

I told Michael about the idea for creating this group and asked about him incorporating the name of his clothing line with the group I wanted to start—he loved that idea. I then got things going creating flyers and driving around the city to get people to come to their first gathering at my house. Unfortunately, the first time only myself and three classmates showed up. We felt down, but not defeated, so I shared the idea with more students and people on campus. In the second meeting, we had six people, which for all of us—was an encouragement to keep trying. We soon expanded to twelve people, than twenty people and I also wanted to bring art to the youth and community.

So, we started reaching out to schools and group homes to help inner-city youth find their healing & escape through art while also giving back to the less fortunate. It became everyone's way of staying positive, healing, and paying it forward. Mike eventually turned the name and carrying out "Jouissance of Expression" to me, promising him to do right by the name. The group grew and flourished with team members, Vice President, and other roles for about five years closing out with a successful open mic night and jam session called "Soulful Sessions" in Rialto, Ca. Jouissance of Expression had come to an end as people moved, had families, and didn't have as much time to commit. However, so many good things happened—that it left a legacy and impact of its own.

Giving my own time to various community advocate causes—as my parents were also activists—led to my following in their footsteps. In my mind, what's the point of doing anything if it isn't for a purpose and it doesn't give back to the community? We all need a village and it's important to utilize our gifts for the greater good. Art as a whole provides healing, unity, a message, and so much more. I use this platform to create a change while accomplishing all of those things. I always take pride in telling a story through art that can deliver that. I do not believe in competition. Instead, I believe we each have a role to play in using our gifts and calling to change the world.

My favorite memory from childhood that I can remember would be learning music and writing from my musically inclined brother and cousin. They were my inspiration and who I looked up to. When 'Lady P' can't get out there to skate with people—you'll catch me enjoying an occasional piggyback ride from one of my skaters to join in on the fun. This exemplifies my love and passion for skating and all it has meant to my life!

ABOUT THE AUTHOR:
Chaz Cunninham Coggins is a national skate DeeJay and one who also hosts DeeJay events in and around California. She has also started her own clothing brand and is doing very well.

Facebook: https://www.facebook.com/DJLadyP
Instagram: @djladyp
www.officialdjladyp.com

QUOTE:
Music is the sound of emotion
Live on Purpose & Love on Purpose

THE ROLLER WAVE

Harry Martin aka Studio 50H

I founded The Roller Wave after unexpectedly having the time of my life at a company party held at LeFrak Center at Lakeside Prospect Park. At the time I hadn't skated since childhood, so it felt like discovering hidden treasure. After going back night after night for an entire summer, I looked for new rinks around the boroughs hoping to find better music and possibly a crowd rooted deeper into authentic skate culture. It was then I found myself in Bed-Stuy at a Salvation Army gym turned part-time makeshift rink. The only thing lacking there was a youthful crowd. I then decided to negotiate my own skate night with the management, bringing out a bevy of promoters, speakers, DJs, and photographers. Roller Wave opened up space to a wider, more diverse audience and after a difference of opinions, I parted ways to look for a space more suitable to my vision.

I then put together a few proposals and shopped them to potential venues with the disclaimer saying, "I know this might sound crazy, but we want to turn your space into a pop-up Roller Disco."

Luckily, The House of Yes in Bushwick was crazy enough to give it a try. I rented the skates for my first event but after facing difficulties with the distributer, I decided that saving every penny of profits from all events and investing in an inventory of roller skates was a better move. Pooling my resources, which was risky at this point because I had a baby on the way—had to be done. The risk paid off in that since June of 2016, The Roller Wave has held thirty-eight sold-out events at The House of Yes and has expanded to The Ludlow House in the Lower East Side, Alpha Space in Crown Heights, Gantry Loft in Long Island City, Soho House in the Meatpacking District, Tao Restaurant for Alicia Key's birthday party, The Williamsburg Hotel with Everyday People, and The Union Square Ballroom. I have even hosted celebrities such as The Bronfman's, Alicia Keys and Swizz Beatz, Mel Gibson, Michael. K. Williams, the Top 100 YouTube Influencers of 2019, and many more.

Now a father and a black small business owner, I can attribute the success of the events to my genuine passion for the culture and respect for the history of Roller Disco alongside the desire to introduce a lost art to a new generation.

I understand roller skating is not a completely lost art—but just in my experience—I have seen a lot that points my opinion in that direction.

Growing up in Crown Heights Brooklyn, I was a frequent flyer at the Empire Roller Skating Rink.

As a toddler, I used to love summer trips and or after-school trips to the rink. I was always practicing at an early age, whether it was how to skate backward, fast, or doing 180-degree jumps. By the time I became a teen, I began visiting Empire Skating Rink every Friday night for their teen night. My first couple of weeks during the teen night, my mom would only let me go if I would let my little brother tag along. Teen night first started as a great party to mingle and skate with peers, but then slowly started to turn into a dance party for teenagers.

As I grew older (fifteen or sixteen years old) pressures of fitting in with peers started to settle in. Fitting in on the streets of Brooklyn, New York in the early 2000s was more like hooking up with the opposite sex, joining street gangs, and hanging with the popular crowds. The popular crowd at the time was more into dancing and wearing the latest fashion. Skating began to die down during teen night at the skating rink (it was like you weren't cool if you were skating at the time). Teens then used the skate floor as a dance floor, which I hated but wanted to fit in, so I chose to not skate anymore.

The day I rediscovered roller skating—back in the year 2015—came at a time when I still to this day, say it was the lowest point of my life. In my late twenties, I felt like life had no direction. Before that event at Le Frak center, I was battling deep depression. I felt like giving up on everything in life, I had no ambitions or cared for myself. During the time, I knew I was dealing with depression, so I became an avid runner. Using running as a tool to battle my depression helped—but did not fully solve the problem.

Going out to the rink every day practicing helped saved my life at the time. I began to equate roller skating to running and how it has very similar benefits but was far more fun and also healthier for the knees and other joints than running. Roller skating became my workouts, I would spend hours getting my cardio on and enjoying old school disco, house, and funk music. I understood how roller skating impacted my life so deeply at the time, so I decided I wanted to be around peers like that to experience this same feeling.

I am currently still hosting roller discos even during the pandemic. When the pandemic started just like everyone else in the world, I began to experience, depression, fear, anxiety and became uninspired. I was scared to go outside. I sat in the house for about two months straight—afraid that I would catch the virus and die.

This feeling I had experienced before in life so I thought to myself, "I will not let this defeat me either."

I began going to the park every day with the thought of building my immune system through fitness so that if I did get sick, I would overcome it. I will not allow anything or anyone to stop me, was my mindset. As I worked out every day in the park, I started seeing a bunch of people in the parks with roller skates. At this point, I was so happy and joyous to see all of the new skaters popping up everywhere. So, I decided to start an outdoor roller-skating series during the pandemic. As it turns out, I brought about two-hundred pairs of skates to the local park and began hosting free roller skate sessions. These outdoor skate sessions, I feel, are one of my biggest accomplishments besides starting the Roller Wave back in 2016.

There are so many testimonies of my peers telling me how it saved their lives during 2020. Just like me, they were coping with a lot of pressures from the pandemic and needed an outlet to feel free and joyous again. I am so happy that I can share my light—with the same wonderful communities I try to have an impact on!

ABOUT THE AUTHOR:

Harry Martin is the Founder of Roller Wave. His concept of a pop- up Roller Disco has taken off, even during the pandemic and he has hosted many sold out events and is continuing to rise. He is married with a small child and resides in New York City. To learn more about the pop up Roller Disco reach out to Harry.

http://www.rollerwavenyc.com/
http://www.instagram.com/rollerwavenyc
http://rollerwavenyc@gmail.com

QUOTE:
"What you do, has a far greater impact than what you say." ~ Steven Covey

A SKATING LOVE STORY

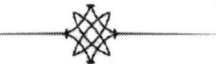

Belinda Dennis-Johnson aka Lady B

Where do I begin
To tell the story of a skating addiction
The sweet love story of a world that used to be
The simple truth about the life it brought to me
Where do I start?

My name is Belinda aka Lady B in the '80s—as named by fellow skaters. I was five-foot-one, and a' hundred pounds of fun like Lady T.

I began skating in 1978. At twenty-three years old, I had just finished my Bachelor's Degree at UC Santa Barbara in '77 and my student teaching at UC Irvine. During this time in my life, I didn't know that I was looking for a new passion. My sister begged me to go with her to the local rink's adult night for about six months...Cypress Skateway.

I remember clearly saying, "No, skating is for kids!"

Finally, I reluctantly decided to try it. "Just once," I thought!

With its first hello
Skating gave meaning to an empty world of mine
There'd never be another love, another time
It came into my world and made the living fine
It filled my heart

I remember the feeling of exhilaration taking my first lap around the rink.

I said to myself, "I will never walk again!"

It felt as natural, sensual, and beautiful—as anything!

My sister didn't skate anymore...I can blame or thank her for my addiction!

[Sidenote: As I look back, that rink was predominantly white with a scattering of people of color. Orange County lies beyond the 'Orange Curtain.' I bring this up because I found myself being more embraced by the African American populations and I can truly look back and feel appreciative of so many people and their love. I was one of the little white girls who could skate!]

At first, I just skated around the rink, tackling backwards skating, but I knew I wanted to learn new steps, including the 'crazy legs and slingshot.' Within the first year, I began checking out other rinks...one or two adult nights per week were not enough for me. I eventually tried Flippers in Hollywood. Those who skated at Flippers know that skating there was not for beginners. We packed into the venue like sardines, so tightly that if one person went down—everyone else was going down. It was one night at Flippers, a man grabbed me from behind and began to skate with me. He was so smooth and our chemistry on the floor was something I never imagined. He told me that he had seen me skate at other rinks and we quickly formed a bond. From then on Phelan Szaabo became my skating partner. We spent countless hours learning, practicing, and teaching.

He taught me to spin and told me "once you get past 'the drunks,' you will be able to spin forever."

He was right. Spinning one hundred times was nothing!

People used to ask Phelan, "How do you get that white girl to move like that?"

He replied, "We just inject her with 10 CCs of soul daily!"

Skating filled my heart with very special things
With angels' songs, with wild imaginings

In 1980, I started teaching at a middle school in Irvine. My life revolved around skating. When I finished work, I would rush home to nap so that I could skate until all hours of the night and still function at work.

Back then there were skating contests. I won my first contest as a singles skater one year after I started skating at the grand opening of Skate Depot in Cerritos.

Phelan informed me that we were going to become the new best skating couple around! Phelan told me about the best couple presently—Tasha and Tony—who had been skating together for years. Their couple's style focused on rexing and ours highlighted on the slingshot. The first contest we were in was The Brass Monkey Roller Showdown. We came in 2nd place to Tasha and Tony, but that was the last time we ever came in 2nd much to the chagrin of haters who often complained that our entry in contests should be illegal—

because no one else had a chance against us. Part of our success was Phelan was an extremely talented tailor/seamster. Our costumes were always amazing.

Because I was spending so much time skating, I decided that I wanted to incorporate it into my teaching career. A fellow teacher taught surfing at Golden West College and put me in touch with the physical education department chair. I wrote a curriculum and a proposal to teach a skating class for college credit. I understood that if I didn't have at least thirty people in the class, it would fall into cancellation. Amazingly enough, I had sixty students!

Golden West College put out a news brief on its new class and the next thing I knew ABC news came out and did a story on me, *Roller Skating Magazine* did an article on me, the *Irvine World News* did an article. I felt like an overnight success! People from all over the United States and Canada were writing to me via *Roller Skating Magazine.*

A funny teaching story.

One morning, my principal walked into my classroom and said, "Hey Dennis…here is what I've been doing with my day. Pulling down pictures of you from the boy's bathroom!"

I was scantily clad in living color skating on the beach on the front page of the *Newport Daily Pilot*. I guess it wasn't very teacher-like behavior! I later asked him why he didn't fire me?

He said, "I saw your potential as a teacher."

For the next several years Phelan and I competed in dance contests in clubs against lockers, break-dancers, and different genres of dancing. We created Roller Jazz Productions and did shows at LA Street Scenes, *Jerry Lewis Telethons*, and performed in schools. We procured a dance studio and people would flock to the dance studio to practice moves before the nightly skating sessions. I had skates on at least eight hours a day. We skated everywhere from Ventura down to San Diego, in clubs, rinks, and even at the beach on the weekend.

In 1981, Skating Plus in Irvine opened. Since I lived in Irvine, I was sure they built the rink for me! There were skating rinks everywhere and an adult night somewhere every night. Skating Plus had the best skating floor around. Irvine residents complained about the 'dark' element coming into their 'lily-white' community. Slowly skating rinks began to close…Laguna Hills Skate Palace, Mission Viejo Skateway, and Irvine Skating Plus. It was much like the story of the movie *Roller Dreams*. White communities complained about the 'element' in their neighborhoods, and law enforcement rolled in, and voila...it was the end of an era.

On a side note, Phelan and I would often skate at Venice Beach, but the music master, (who will remain unnamed) was often angry about the attention we got and would turn the music off. We found our following at other beaches and brought our music. The skating world has many big egos!

We also experienced many doses of prejudice. One night after we performed at a club in Santa Monica, the police lit up sirens, pulling us over —and insisted on tearing my car apart to look for drugs. Black men in the car, in their mind, equated to 'there must be drugs.'

Roller Jazz Productions was hiring to promote Billy Barty's skating rink in Fullerton was a win-win for us—after we slam-dunked the contest in both couples and singles. One night we were passing out flyers at World on Wheels in Los Angeles.

We asked the manager for permission to hand out the flyers and he said, "As long as you stay on the sidewalk which is public property."

There were three sidewalk exits, Phelan, another friend, and I each took an exit. The security guard came up to us and informed us that we were not allowed to pass out the flyers. We informed him that we had permission from the manager. He informed us that he was the manager of the outside and what the manager inside said was wrong. We went on about our business of passing out flyers. The next thing I knew the security guard ran up on me, put me in a headlock, and dragged me over to a pole handcuffing me to it. Thus, making an example out of me—in front of the skating rink for all to see. This rent-a-cop-brut then went inside to get the manager—and show him his captive little white girl! (Note: He didn't take either of the guys!) The manager came out and reprimanded the security guard and set me free. Traumatized, the guys took me to the local police station to report an assault. I never returned to World on Wheels until twenty years later and I still felt traumatized.

Sadly in 1984, Phelan and I ended our skating partnership. Continuing with Roller Jazz Productions, I hired the Venice Skaters to perform in various shows we still had contractual obligations with including LA Street Scenes—which featured in the motion picture *Roller Dreams*. I skated with another partner who came in from Arizona. He was a great skater, but the skating chemistry just wasn't the same.

I began branching out my performances to include dance and joined a Prince lip-syncing dance group and it just so happened that a show was MC'd by Muhammed Ali. I had an agent who was also Muhammed Ali's agent and after the show, my agent told me that Mr. Ali had invited me to come to his house. My skating career had led me to the home of Muhammad Ali in Hancock Park. The next day I found myself sitting across the desk from one of the greatest athletes of our time. He was kind and gracious. We didn't carry around cameras back then and it is one of my greatest regrets that I did not take a picture with him.

In 1985, the opportunity arose for me to dance on *Soul Train*. For the next three years, I incorporated *Soul Train* into my repertoire. My students would dance into the classroom on Monday mornings singing *The Soul Train* theme after they saw me on the show. I skated constantly but felt incomplete without a skating partner. Many asked me to partner with them, but no one had the skills of Phelan. He disappeared from the skating circuit.

In 1988, another fantastic opportunity to skate came up—the Super Bowl halftime show!

Cooley Jackson one of the Lockers whom I had previously competed against choreographed the show. Cooley, Caszper, and Jeffrey Daniels were street dancers who taught Michael Jackson the Moonwalk.

Performing in the halftime show was euphoria. I remember running through the tunnel, onto the field, and across the 100yds in my skates. I turned around and the field yielded to over fifty beautiful baby grand pianos and the Rockettes. There were eight discs on the field, and eight skaters lifted by local San Diego high school football players—set in motion—as we skated to Chubby Checker, the main performer. At the time I was five months pregnant with my first child. We practiced for three days before the show and on the 3rd day, the boys asked me if I was pregnant.

It was very cute when they shyly said, "We couldn't figure out why you are in such good shape, but you have a belly!"

The following weekend, I went back to record on *Soul Train* and the choreographer asked me if I was pregnant. He told me to come back again after I delivered. I never went back to dance, but I returned socially with my baby and still do *Soul Train* events on occasion including being in parades and attending reunions.

How long does it last?

Can a passion be measured by the hours in a day?
I have no answers now but this much I can say
I know my love of skating will never burn away
And my memories will always be right there
Within my heart

After the birth of my daughter, Karissa, and then two sons, DeRon and Jerrick, I seldom skated. My husband wasn't a fan of my skating career.

Because I don't let the grass grow under my feet, I decided to work on a Master's Degree in Counseling Psychology in 1992. Becoming licensed in 1999 paid off—after years of interning on the side and sitting for my written and oral exams. My life consisted of raising kids, being a football team mom, and cheerleading performances.

In 2002, after many years of an unhappy marriage, I filed for divorce and got my skates back out even though I was 47. The community welcomed me back with open arms and I was skating with quite a few of the skaters of yesteryear—who were around my age. A new style of skating had evolved, based on a step called 'downtown.' Once again, I found myself craving my life on skates and learning new steps. I have always enjoyed skating in the middle and doing routines with other skaters. Even as I began dating, I wasn't interested in spending time with anyone unless it didn't cut into my skate night!

I retired from teaching in 2010. I had already started a private practice as a psychotherapist in 2004. I named my practice InnerVisions Therapeutic Solutions (after lyrics from Lady T and Stevie Wonder) and it had grown enough for me to take early retirement. Little did I know, my practice would explode. I began spending more time growing a business once again and eventually less time skating.

In the era of Black Lives Matter and as the mother of Black children, I truly appreciate the way Black culture has always welcomed me in. I have my own experiences with prejudice, but I am beyond blessed to consider people of all races my sisters and brothers.

My bonus daughter, Jasmin, who is now grown with her own family found *Roller Dreams* in May of 2020. She called me to tell me that I was in the movie. She proceeded to send me clips of a movie produced in 2017 that I knew nothing about.

In late 2019, I began beating myself up for not skating as much as I should. Deciding in favor of starting to balance my life and incorporate skating more—the virus known as COVID-19 struck. Will we ever be able to enjoy the golden moments in a skating rink again? I don't know, but my passion for skating will never die.

How long does it last
Can skate life be measured by the hours we have rolled
I have no answers now but this much I can say
I know I'll need to skate 'till the stars all burn away
And if there is a rink, I will be there!

ABOUT THE AUTHOR:

Belinda led a pretty sheltered life as a child and was not allowed to go to skating rinks. Her parents had concerns that 'old men' hung around skating rinks. LOL! Skating around the block here and there with some old-fashioned skates was her only skating experience, but rinks were out of the question. Belinda moved out and age eighteen wanting independence and put herself through college. She graduated early at age seventeen and received a four-year degree at age twenty-one. When asked to go skating after college, she resisted, thinking skating was for kids. BOY WAS SHE WRONG!

Currently, Belinda is a retired teacher and in private practice as a psychotherapist.

QUOTE:
"I used to be a queen you know
On an island by the sea
With rainbow-colored people
Happy as can be
Never had a problem
There never was a care
And love was ever-flowing and it's feeling shared" Lyrics by Teena Marie (*DeJaVu*)

Facebook: @Belinda Dennis-Johnson
Instagram: @innervisions07

ROLLER, ROCKER, REVIEW

Linwood D. Neverson

Roller Skating for me started in 1976, at Empire Roller Rink in Brooklyn, New York. I come from a family of roller skaters. My uncle founded the **'8 Ball & the Blue Guerillas'** in 1971, and another uncle worked as a floor guard, DJ, and security guard. My immediate family and my cousins all skated too.

Being a child from a family of skaters, had its privileges. The first time I went skating, it was a 7 to 7 session. The DJ was Grand Master Flowers and the music was pumping. I can remember being eye level with the railing, as I held on to pull myself around the rink. My uncle skated up to me, pulled me from the railing, took me to the middle of the rink—and left me there. My life was forever changed. I had become a serial roller skater.

From 1976-1983 I skated in rinks, all up and down the East Coast with the **Blue Guerillas**. We would jump in that van, and visit a rink where we could go and represent Empire and Brooklyn. I loved going to Twin City. They had one of the biggest rinks on the East Coast.

My style of skating was more of a rider. I loved the speed. I would get to the outside of that rink and would skate all night long. I learned how to do trains & trios, and partner skating at a very young age from the adults in the rink. Getting on those trains with some of the legends was so exhilarating and so much fun.

My family moved to Long Island from Brooklyn and I was not able to get to the rinks as much as I would have liked. As I was getting older, I started hanging out in the streets more, and the rinks less. I soon found myself in a situation that almost cost me my life. Shot four times—they left me to die in the streets.

While I was recovering, all I could think about was healing, so that I could get back to the rink.

In the rink, I found peace and solace. It was a safe place where I could think, be creative, be myself, and release my abundance of energy. I replaced the streets with the rink—and life was rolling along.

I met my ex-wife at Lacey. I got married, had two beautiful daughters

Khira and Jair. I worked, raised my daughters, and I continued to roller skate.

In 2007, Empire Roller Rink was closing its doors forever. To document this monumental event, I pulled out my video camera. I studied Film Production at Brooklyn College. This was my chance to do two things I loved to do. Shoot and Skate. For that entire week, I went to Empire and I captured the pain, the joy, the sadness, the spins, slides, trains, and trios. I captured roller skaters in their element; it was the place where they felt most free and at home.

When Empire closed, I felt like the skate community was giving up and quitting. I felt like a piece of my past, present, and future—was leaving me. As the lights came on after the last skate, hundreds of skaters stood around and talked. There were tears, laughter, and a lot of reminiscing already taking place about some of the amazing events that occurred at the infamous Empire Roller Rink.

For the first time, I listened to other people's stories about why they love skating and why they needed to skate. There were so many backgrounds, cultures, similarities, and differences. The roller skating rink was truly a melting pot and the richness of the stories filled my spirit. I realized that for years, I skated amongst strangers and now I had a strong desire to hear their stories. That night, the idea to create and produce the documentary *Just Skate*, was born. This documentary will capture the names, stories, and life lessons from talented and gifted skaters across the country to learn why we love to skate.

Since 2008, I have been traveling and filming National Skate events all over the country. I have more than 100 interviews from Skate Legends, OG Skaters, and the New Generation Skaters.

I am the founder of Sk8Kingz Media, and we are in the Post Production phases of the documentary, *Just Skate*. It will showcase the talent and expertise of just some of the magnificent skaters from the New York and New Jersey areas.

To honor the legends and those skaters that have contributed a major footprint to the skate community, I co-produced **The Legends Gala** and the **Capital Skate Fest** in Washington DC in 2019 with Saletta Coleman. This by far is one of the most memorable, elegant, and impactful events that I have ever attended. We skated thirty-one stories in the air, overlooking the Lincoln Memorial as skaters from all over the country—elegantly decked out in gowns, tuxedos, and top hats—all skated the night away.

God continues to bless me, and I am truly honored to be a skate videographer because I get to capture skaters while they are in their zone. I can show the skaters and the world the beauty, finesse, individuality, and showmanship of thousands of talented skaters. I get to capture poetry in motion from the inside of the rink and magnify the voices of the skaters to bring a clear understanding as to why, we absolutely, and unequivocally—are obsessed—and have to put our '8 Wheels on the Floor!'

ABOUT THE AUTHOR:

Linwood D. Neverson is from Uniondale, New York, and is the founder of **Sk8Kingz_Media**. He has been skating for over forty years. He is currently directing and producing the documentary *Just Skate*, which will feature multiple generations of skaters from around the country and highlight the one thing they all have in common—their love for skating. The goal of this project is to pay forward the love and the cultivation of skating—as it was passed down to Mr. Neverson.

With all the things he seeks to accomplish, he does it with the understanding that Jesus Christ is his Lord and Savior, and through him—all things are possible.

Instagram: @Sk8Kingz_Media
Facebook: @Sk8Kingz
www.Sk8Kingz.com

QUOTE:

All things through Christ who strengthens me.

IN MEMORIUM

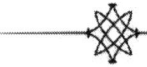

Sending peace and prayers to those in the skate world whom we have lost but whom shall never be forgotten:

Atlanta
Zach Boothby
Shawn "Trump" Walker
Erica Moten

Delaware
Adrea "Dre" Garrett

Illinois
Preciise Davis

Michigan
Theresa Jones
Mr. Melvin Jones
Judy Spradley

Minnesota
Baxter "Dollar Bill" Davis

New Jersey
Chuck Goins Sr. – New Jersey
Lloyd "Old Man Pops" Brown

New Orleans
Kathy Hinyard

New York City
Lezly Ziering
Clarice Boo Honey Mustard
Crazy Eddie Campos
Little Mike Johnson
Will Reid – NYC
Carlos Sanchez

Ohio
Norman Carr Cinny
DJ Jim Dandy Cinny
Jarel "Mello" Jones
James Foster
Lil Darrell Farr
Joe Bass

Oregon
Nick Roberts

Pennsylvania
Larry Clark
Willie Garrett
Tracey Coleman
Reggie Coleman
Morris "Philly Flash" Armstrong

Rhode Island
Ricky Young

Virginia
Ed "Hitman" Harris

International
Canada
Morgan Henry – Canada

Correction from Vol I: Lakiesha (Redbone) Tillman
For those not mentioned, you will forever be in our hearts, prayers and in our souls with each roll of our wheels.

THIS IS MY STORY, MY LOVE STORY A TRIBUTE TO LEZLY ZIERING

Written by Robbin Ziering in Memorium of Lezly Ziering

A man named Lezly Ziering, my late and great husband, this is for you, may you RIP in sk8ers heaven!

I used to be a rollerblader and I went all around Central Park on those blades, it took a while to gather up the courage to go down those steep hills in the back of the park but I got it and after a year or two, it became too easy, I was not learning anymore, I was bored. I decided to cut across the 72nd Street transverse instead of going all the way around on a sunny, warm Sunday afternoon, I am an RN and a dancer. I heard some great music so I headed in that direction and I came across the craziest party scene I'd ever seen. hundreds of people from every walk of life dancing to the beat of a live DJ on, what? Are those old-fashioned roller skates? What? I never saw so many people having so much fun in my life. I said to myself, "I can skate, blade, I can dance, that's my life!" I was forty years old and I knew I just found my world, my identity, and the people to who I would forever belong.

I skated in on those blades and I asked, "What was this?"

This man said, "Welcome to the Central Park Skate Circle!"

The skaters amazed me, the moves they made to the beat of the music, making it all look so easy. I asked this skater where can I learn this.

He looked down at my blades and said "not on those."

I said, "So where do I get those?"

He said, "Lezly"

I said, "And who can teach me?"

He said, "Lezly."

I said, "Who's Lezly?"

He said, "Lezly founded this place."

I replied, "Where was he?"

The man told me he wasn't there yet but would be arriving shortly.

I asked him if he would tell me when he arrived and he said, "NO!"

I asked why.

He said, "YOU WILL KNOW!"

I replied, "How will I know?"

He said, "You will feel it!"

"What will I feel?" I said.

"You'll know!" The man replied.

Therefore, I sat on a bench, my back toward the entrance.

I thought he was just kidding. I waited about five minutes and suddenly,

I felt a surge, it was like a sigh as if this crazy-ass crowd of skaters was breathing a sigh of relief, "he's here," I thought I heard.

I asked the same man, "He's here, isn't he?"

"Yes, he's walking in right now!"

Wow! This man's smile lit up the world and his eyes reflected a sense of kindness that you couldn't miss if you tried, these eyes that filled a room with love and happiness! He was like magic. As he passed thru to the middle with his backpack with his skates and wheeling his bike, he was being greeted like a Rockstar by everybody. I waited a moment until he got to the DJ booth and I approached with such excitement.

"Hi, Lezly? My name is Robbin and as you can see I rollerblade but I also dance and Oh My God, would you please help me purchase these skates and teach me all this?"

He put on his deepest funniest voice and said, "Why of course!"

He had such a teasing twinkle in his eyes. I knew we would become fast friends but I never knew exactly how I had predicted that I had found my life the way I did! Lezly got me my skates and we set off to teach me real skating. We had such an easy way of relating and interacting with each other. He knew I was serious about learning how to dance on skates so he went about the business of taking me under his thumb and he paid close attention to teaching me.

He introduced me to the skaters in the Park, he knew that I would one day become part of them. He taught me outdoors then he brought me to his indoor classes at the Roxy, a nightclub except for two nights a week that he negotiated to open for skating. It was magic. I felt it in the air, like the park. He introduced me to his circle of friends where they sat in these oval-shaped booths reminiscent of a scene from a 1950s movie. His friends were hysterically funny and raucous. When he was on the floor he weaved in and out, and between the skaters with such ease, his graceful abilities were stunning.

Lezly was a famous dancer also as it turned out, he was the only male featured dancer in a Gene Kelly movie, Gene Kelly directed it and chose not to dance, Lezly collaborated Natalie Wood in it, and *Marjorie Morningstar* came forth! Lezly also had just closed his dance and skate school. To this day I meet strangers who introduce themselves to me to speak of this space they called home, a place that breathed on its own and people describe that it gave them life. They lived and slept there; they could not get enough.

So far, there was nothing I saw that was not just pure magic, and Lezly and I were soon in the throes of a great friendship as I progressed in my dance skate skills.

For me, ours was a wonderful friendship between two magnificent human beings of limitless gifts. I would watch him partnering with other ladies in awe. How do they do that? Soon he began to teach me how to skate with a partner but it was during the skate session and he didn't want to miss what the skaters call their quality skate time. I had to learn just by baby steps but I watched closely and I learned a lot by doing that. The ladies always waiting for their chance to skate with him and he was so kind as to never turn a lady down. Lezly didn't have a nasty bone in his body. He could never hurt anyone's feelings. He never turned a back, ignored, or said no to any lady. Lezly was only about love, kindness, happiness and it was as if his arms were open and welcoming to anybody who wanted to come in.

Still, he was my good friend and teacher, we were having a great time together but so was everyone else. I did not feel I was more special than anyone else, I just felt a part of this special man's life. I found my life, the one I searched for forty years and would have been happy just being in that moment forever.

One night a friend of Lezly told me he sees the way Lezly looked at me and he thought Lezly might be falling for me.

I just laughed and said, "No we're just really good friends," then disaster struck, I have Cystic Fibrosis, I rarely spoke of it.

I got pneumonia and needed a ventilator, I thought it was the end of my newly found friends. Skaters will not want to be hanging around someone as sick as I was, sick people, are supposed to be too needy. But instead, Lezly came from downtown to uptown twice a day to feed my cats and sit by my bedside until I was out of my drug-induced coma and off life support. I was stunned by how loyal my friend was, how he cared so deeply. But he cared deeply for everyone so I still just assumed he was just the best friend I ever had.

My parents came to visit and they said he loved me.

"No!" I proclaimed, "We were just good friends, how could a man of his stature love me?"

Well, I was wrong, we became better friends, and we had benefits now! He always told me he would always be a bachelor and he never wanted to hurt me so if I could not deal with it, I should move on. I felt I could deal with it. I wasn't looking to get married either and I loved my place so I didn't feel I needed to live with him. I had it all, no commitments but still I felt loved and I was falling head over heels but still I wanted my independence too. We had a lot in common, it worked.

One day, unexpectedly, Lezly asked me if I would move in with him. He told me he missed me so much when he went home. I was torn, I loved him but I also loved my space, I had to think about it. Our friends were thinking "girl are you nuts?" Lezly persisted and I began missing him when he went home, so off I went on a new adventure. I moved in, we were both in love and didn't want to be apart. As I have gotten to know him more intimately, I realized how humble a man he was, he never boasted of his successes, I found out in little segments about his accomplishments but usually from other people. He was not presumptuous but surprised by the attention he got. I remember always standing a step behind—as it was not my glory—it was his.

Lezly always told me he would never get married but would remain true to me. I am not a jealous or possessive person. If I ever felt, I could not trust a man, I always preferred just to move on.

Lezly and I grew more in love. Soon, to me, he wasn't that icon anymore, he became just Lezly, this man I loved. I remained just Robbin, never Robbin who was loved by a man who was known as an icon! I always remained true to myself. I think Lezly respected that about me. I was only impressed that we loved each other equally on the same level.

Nevertheless, he always maintained, "Never say the M-word, MARRIAGE!" I did not.

We were driving on the FDR parkway one day and he pulled over. I asked him why he was pulling over. He said if he said what he was going to say while he was driving, we would have an accident. I thought the worst, it was over or he was sick but whatever it was could not have been good.

He said, "Robbin I'm so in love with you if you don't marry me, I'll just die!" I decided to play him for a moment, I love to play. Therefore, I sat there and pondered and then turned to him and saw he was a little worried, waiting for my reply. I said, "Only if we can do it on skates!" There it was that deep hearty laugh and we sealed the deal with a kiss.

Therefore, it was done and what a wedding it was. Three hundred screaming skaters. When he rolled down the Roxy floor to the Alter, a roar from the crowd went up. I turned to leave; I thought, "I'll be so embarrassed, they'll never roar for me!" It was my turn, I hesitated. I saw him looking like, where is she. I took a deep breath and stepped on the floor—and they roared. Nobody ever roared for me! It took my breath away. I always knew how special he was to everybody—but this drove it home.

Lezly was so entertaining, he had a high genius IQ but he did not have to tell that to anybody, he used his genius to wordplay on people.

He said, "Duny, now please if you are reading this don't say it, you won't be able to, and even though he's gone the earth will quake."

But I did say it back to him exactly how he pronounced it, he became Duny forever. He was so worried if I said it in public people would try to call him Duny and mispronounce it but I always knew they would just know it was our thing as was Nibbor and I was right for the rest of our lives together we were Duny and Nibbor, nobody dared venture there. He changed "love" to "Vole" now instead of saying "I love you Robbin" it became "Vole Nibbor" and I would always respond "Vole Duny"

My most awesome memory was that after about three or maybe four years this man who only considered other women his skate partners but still worked diligently with me to strictly, but with love, teach me how to partner him and me always asking him "did I skate good tonight Duny?"

He replied, "No you skated well." After asking several weeks in a row why he always answered me that way, he said, "Robbin you do 'good' things and you do things well!"

I started to correct myself and to this day when I hear someone say the "good" word instead of the "well" word I cringe.

However, one of those days when we were coming home, he said, "Nibbor you are skating so well now that I consider you to be my partner!"

I went nuts! How could I ever have accomplished such a feat but I did and I knew it, we were one with the universe now when we skated together. I saw the expressions on the skater's faces. He wowed the ladies! The ladies were begging for at least one skate a night and that was fine with me, I loved sharing Lezly with the world. I knew he loved me. I gave him my blessings with all the love in my heart. I will never forget how I skated with Lezly and how I have never partnered with another man since.

When Lezly became ill he finally accepted his fate after a bad fall, he looked up at me and said: "Nibbor that was my last fall, I'm going to die."

I knew he was right with my nursing eyes. As we lay on the floor, me holding him until the ambulance came, I promised to take care of him at home for the rest of his life and a song came to mind, it went like this, I sang to him.

> Stay with me, stay with me
> Spend just one more day with me
> I cannot bear to see it end this way...
>
> If I could spend one night with you, it would last my whole night through
> In addition, of all the nights I need the most, tonight's the night that means the most
> I never thought that I could meet someone so beautiful,
> Never thought I'd see a night like this
> Because when you know you're going to lose someone so beautiful
> For the rest of your life, that's an awful lot to live
> So won't you stay with me
> Oh, stay with me... --Diana Ross

And so it goes, RIP DUNY! I love you with every beat of my heart!
Now I don't love to skate, I skate to live!
THANK YOU FOR THE RIDE OF MY LIFE, YOU WERE EVERYTHING AND MORE!
I THANK YOU FROM THE BOTTOM OF MY HEART,
VOLE DUNY, RIP!

Just to note, he died late on a Wednesday night, the following Sunday my aunt called and told me to go get the Sunday New York Times, she would not say why. When I came home, I called and told her to spill it. She told me to go to the obit.

He made the entire page of the Sunday New York Times obituary page.

LIST OF AUTHORS IN CHAPTER ORDER

1. Charles Edwards
2. Khannie Butler
3. Lisa Campolo Goodheart
4. Jeff Hart
5. Israel Strong
6. Terry Davis
7. Joanne Fountaine
8. Maurice Sanders
9. Bryant Harvey
10. Kevin Williams
11. Temptest Hall
12. Sara Messenger
13. Richard Manning
14. Lukki Jermaine
15. Stacey Davis
16. Jim Krummenacker
17. Sam Fonville
18. Patricia Bush
19. Kenny Davis
20. Kris Ward
21. Mitchell Verley
22. Chaz Cunningham Coggins
23. Harry Martin
24. Belinda Dennis-Johnson
25. Linwood D. Neverson
26. Robbin Ziering

Made in the USA
Monee, IL
24 July 2022